CHURCHES OF GREATER MANCHESTER

ROB ANDREWS

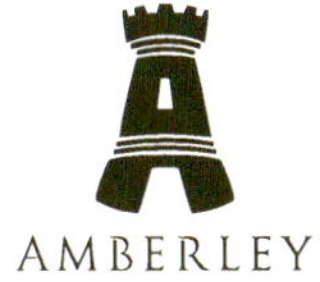

AMBERLEY

This edition first published 2026

Amberley Publishing
The Hill, Stroud
Gloucestershire GL5 4EP

www.amberley-books.com

British Library Cataloguing in Publication Data.
A catalogue record for this book is available from the British Library.

ISBN 978 1 3981 2371 7 (print)
ISBN 978 1 3981 2372 4 (ebook)

Typesetting by SJmagic DESIGN SERVICES, India.
Printed in Great Britain.

Appointed GPSR EU Representative: Easy Access System Europe Oü, 16879218
Address: Mustamäe tee 50, 10621, Tallinn, Estonia
Contact Details: gpsr.requests@easproject.com, +358 40 500 3575

CONTENTS

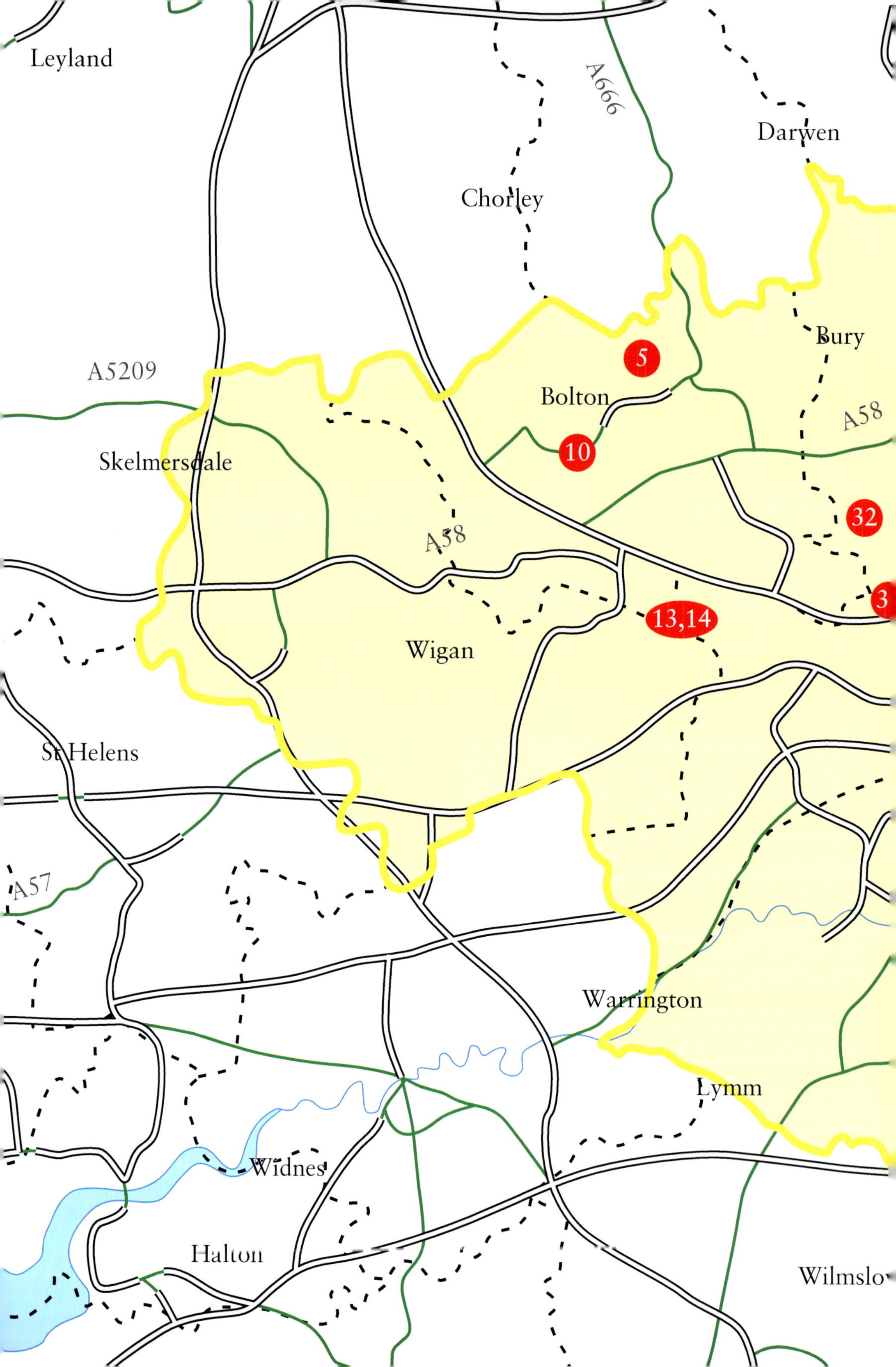

Leyland
A666
Darwen
Chorley
Bury
5
A5209
Bolton
A58
10
Skelmersdale
32
A58
3
13,14
Wigan
St Helens
A57
Warrington
Lymm
Widnes
Halton
Wilmslo

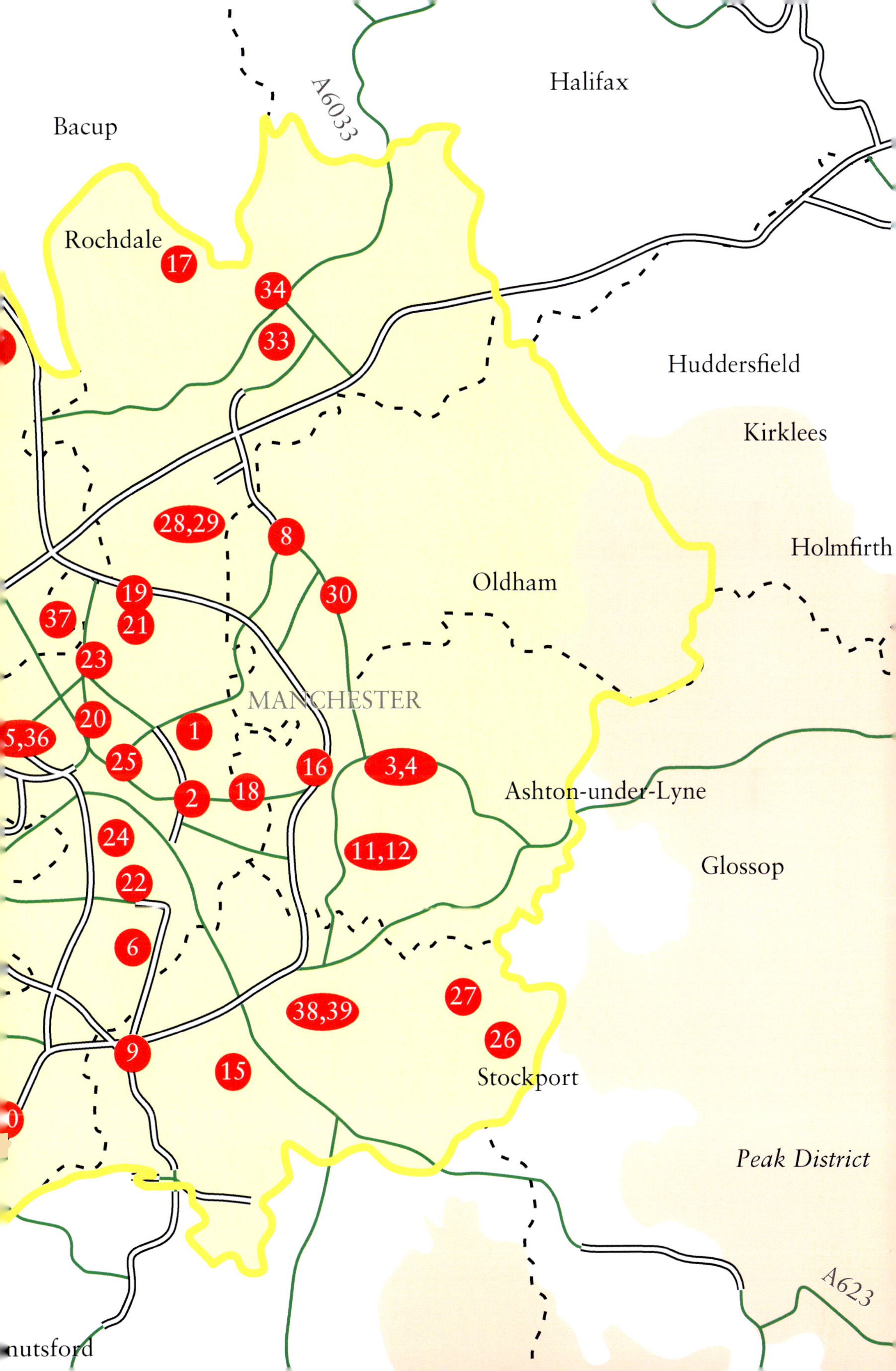

Halifax
Bacup
Rochdale
17
34
33
A6033
Huddersfield
Kirklees
Holmfirth
28,29
8
30
Oldham
19
37
21
23
MANCHESTER
20
1
5,36
25
16
3,4
2
18
Ashton-under-Lyne
24
11,12
Glossop
22
6
38,39
27
26
9
15
Stockport
0
Peak District
nutsford
A623

Key

1. Ancoats, Hallé St Peter's
2. Ardwick, St Benedict
3. Ashton, St James
4. Ashton-under-Lyne, St Michael and All Angels
5. Bolton, All Souls
6. Burnage, St Nicholas
7. Bury, St Mary
8. Chadderton, St Mark
9. Cheadle, St Mary
10. Deane, St Mary
11. Denton, St Anne (Haughton)
12. Denton, St Lawrence
13. Eccles, St Andrew
14. Eccles, St Mary
15. Edgley, St Matthew
16. Fairfield Moravian Church
17. Falinge, St Edmund
18. Gorton Monastery
19. Manchester, High Blackley, St Clare
20. Manchester, St Mary (Mulberry Street)

21. Manchester Cathedral
22. Manchester, The Holy Name of Jesus
23. Manchester, St Ann
24. Manchester, St Augustine
25. Manchester, St Peter's Cross
26. Marple, All Saints
27. Low Marple, St Martin
28. Middleton, St Leonard
29. Middleton, St Michael
30. Oldham Parish Church (St Mary and St Peter)
31. Prestwich, St Mary
32. Radcliffe, St Mary
33. Rochdale, St Chad
34. Rochdale, St Mary in the Baum
35. Salford Cathedral
36. Salford, St Philip
37. Salford, Sacred Trinity
38. Stockport, St Mary
39. Stockport, St Peter
40. Wythenshawe, William Temple Church

Introduction

Greater Manchester is often perceived as a region with few examples of historic churches of architectural significance, and even fewer still that are regularly accessible to the public outside of service times. Subsequently, they have received little attention in the pages of popular guides on the subject of exploring our nation's great ecclesiastical built heritage. Author Simon Jenkins once commented that 'visiting the churches of south Lancashire demands an adventurous spirit'. In my experience of visiting churches across the Greater Manchester area, of which south and south-east Lancashire form a part, there is some truth to his comment. However, this should not deter the reader from exploring Greater Manchester and visiting its wonderful churches; they will be rewarded for doing so.

Manchester had been a centre for nearby wool merchants in the surrounding Pennine landscape since the medieval period. It was during the eighteenth century that a sudden growth in industry emerging from Manchester spread to the cotton mill towns to the north. A short time later, the area we call Greater Manchester today had almost entirely moved away from its rural beginnings, with residents previously working on farms having adapted to a new way of life marked by industry and commerce.

Nowadays, the rapid urban growth of Manchester city centre is defined by radical redevelopment, but the city is also celebrated for its rich industrial heritage, and the central streets boast some of the finest examples of muscular civic and commercial Victorian architecture in the north of England. Additionally, the city is of appeal to the more discerning visitors in search of its great Victorian ecclesiastical buildings.

There is in fact a great variation in date and architectural style of the churches in Greater Manchester. The surviving medieval churches in the area do not, for the most part, retain substantial amounts of their pre-Reformation building fabric when compared to neighbouring counties, usually due to phases of later rebuilding. There were once only seven ancient parishes, reflecting, as art historian Nikolaus Pevsner pointed out, 'the sparseness of the population'. Manchester and Rochdale were the largest. On account of their etymology, Eccles and Prestwich were perhaps the most significant in ecclesiastical terms. The remaining of the ancient parishes were Middleton, Oldham, Bury and Bolton. Very few complete buildings predating the Reformation have survived in the Greater Manchester area, and this is especially true of Manchester itself.

Manchester has lost many of its Georgian churches as well. Only St Ann's Church remains today from a busy period of church building during the expansion of the old town in the eighteenth century, standing at one end of St Ann's Square to the south of the heart of Manchester's medieval core. St Ann's stands testament to a period of rapid expansion and development during the second half of the eighteenth century, with the last of the 'lost churches' being demolished in 1977. Street names dotted around the city centre refer back to the dedications of Anglican churches which once stood nearby. Resonances of Manchester's past remain in the ever-changing centre but are increasingly challenging to pinpoint.

The rapid expansion of Manchester, its neighbouring post-industrial towns and their suburbs have provided a context for a great number of modernist churches which deserve to be more widely appreciated. Within Manchester, the expanding residential areas required new, more permanent churches and there are several examples of buildings from more established architects, such as George G. Pace, through to those deserving of greater study, such as the Manchester-based architect Tom. D. Howcroft, designer of several Nonconformist churches and chapels around Greater Manchester. It is not common for new church buildings to be built today, at least not in the Anglican tradition. However, between 2002 and 2003 a new church was built in the name of the Intercession of the Holy Virgin for the Russian Orthodox Church in the diocese of Sourozh.

Church closure and subsequent changes of use mean some significant church buildings are now no longer active places of worship. In some cases, these buildings that had previously been neglected have been restored and adapted. Public access is permitted to these buildings, and several are included in this book.

This book is not a gazetteer of every important church in Greater Manchester, nor is it an exhaustive survey of every church from a particular period of history. The scope of the buildings included reflects the heritage of Anglican, Roman Catholic and Nonconformist worship in the area and their presence in local communities, with specific attention given to re-orderings and in some cases where the church has closed, a change of use. It is hoped that the reader will now have some idea not only of the magnificent art and architecture to be found in the churches of Greater Manchester, but also of their great social and historical significance.

1. Ancoats, Hallé St Peter's

St Peter's was built in 1859 to designs by architect Isaac Holden, the founding chairman of the Manchester Society of Architects. Consecrated the following year, St Peter's was the first Anglican church to be built in the predominantly Roman Catholic community of Ancoats in central Manchester. The church was built on a tight budget in brick, which was considerably cheaper than stone, with cast-iron columns to support the arches between the nave and aisles.

There was no pew rent due to the area being so poor.

The size of the congregation was diminishing by the 1950s and became unsustainable prior to the church closing for regular worship in 1960. The building was abandoned in the early 1990s and left to deteriorate as time passed until 1995 when the Ancoats Buildings Preservation Trust was established. They coordinated a major repair effort to restore the roofs and high-level brickwork. Work to restore St Peter's was complete by 2003 with aid of a grant from the Heritage Lottery Fund, as well as English Heritage and the Architectural Heritage Fund. The church was gutted of its remaining interior fittings and the former church is now a permanent rehearsal centre and a resource for the whole community.

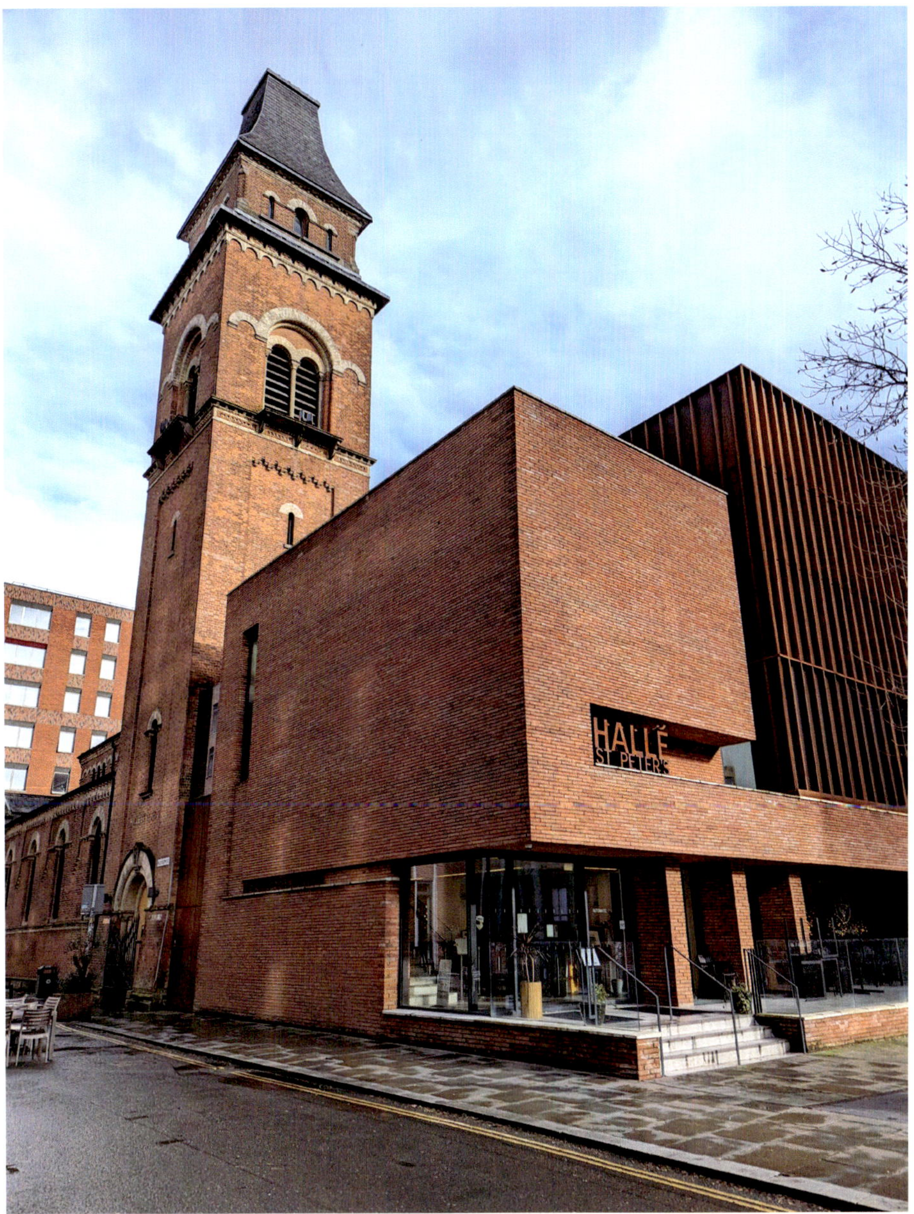

Hallé St Peter's, Ancoats.

2. Ardwick, St Benedict

Joseph Stretch Crowther designed several church buildings in the Gothic Revival style across Greater Manchester. Collectively, they can be seen to share some overlapping characteristics, such as wide-aisled central worship spaces with the proportions of great halls, high-set windows and soaring towers in various forms. Of Crowther's buildings that have survived demolition or closure in the Greater Manchester area, perhaps the most magnificent is St Benedict's Church in Ardwick,

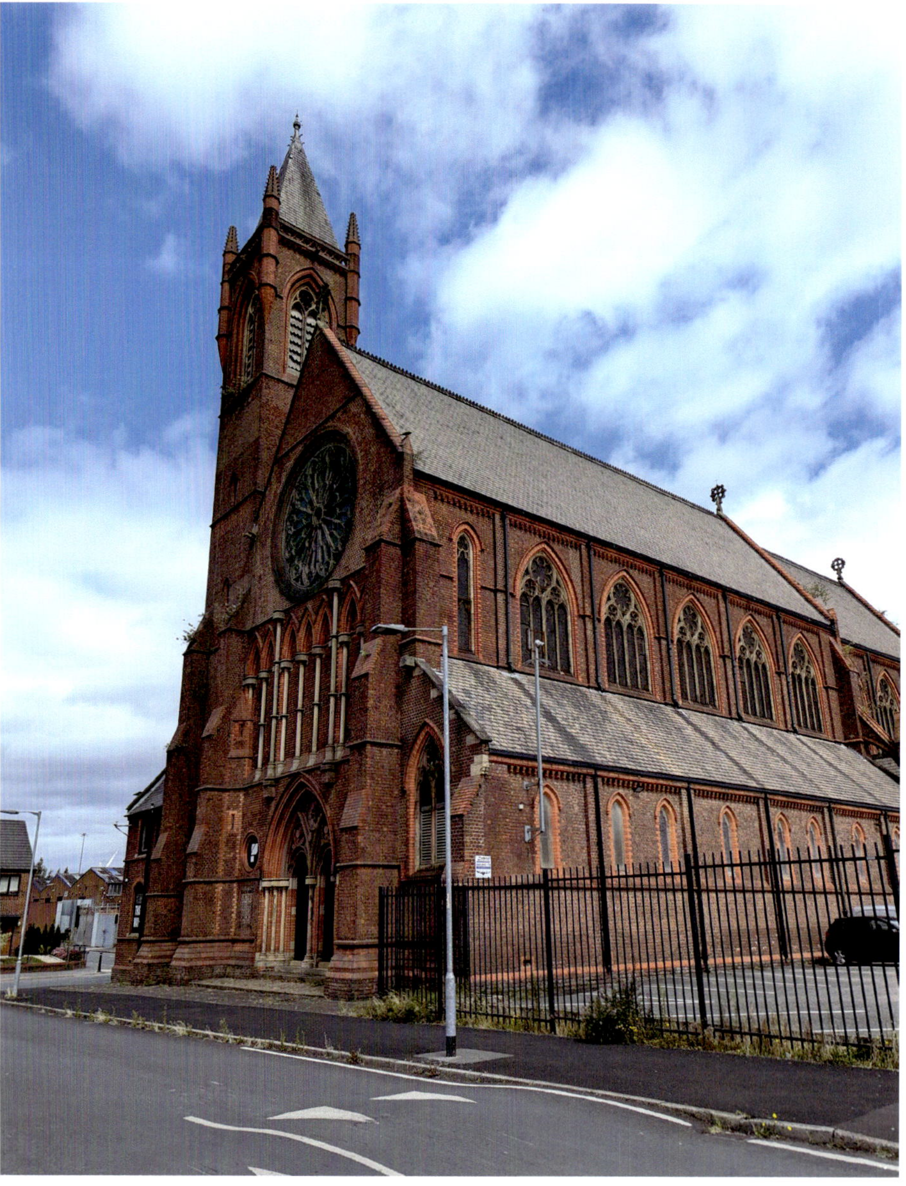

Church of St Benedict, Ardwick.

built in 1880. This is not a church dressed completely in stone, but one faced externally in red brick with orange brick dressings and stone tracery, giving it a pleasant polychrome effect. In proportion alone, the church could be mistaken for a factory or mill building and dwarfs all other buildings in the vicinity. The various architectural components of the west façade are unmistakably Early English Gothic in style, flanked with a distinguished, Italianate north-west tower. There are three stages to the elevation of the west façade, beginning with an arched doorway of three orders of moulded brick voussoirs and a traceried tympanum of red sandstone. Above this is a band of fairly plain blind arcading. The rose window is a triumph, also Italianate and in the wheel style, although it cannot be fully appreciated as it is covered with a protective mesh, dulling its appearance. When Ardwick was terraced and had a larger residential population, services at St Benedict's were well attended, but the church was formally closed in the early 2000s and was home to Parthian Climbing Manchester, formerly the Manchester Climbing Centre, until its closure on 29 July 2025. Luckily, I was able to inspect the building prior to this date, and the following description records a visit from the previous year.

One of the difficulties facing developers when considering whether to take on closed Anglican churches specifically is what to do with the quite unique and separate internal spaces. Naves and chancels are seldom unified spaces. In traditional church architecture, they are generally separated by a change in

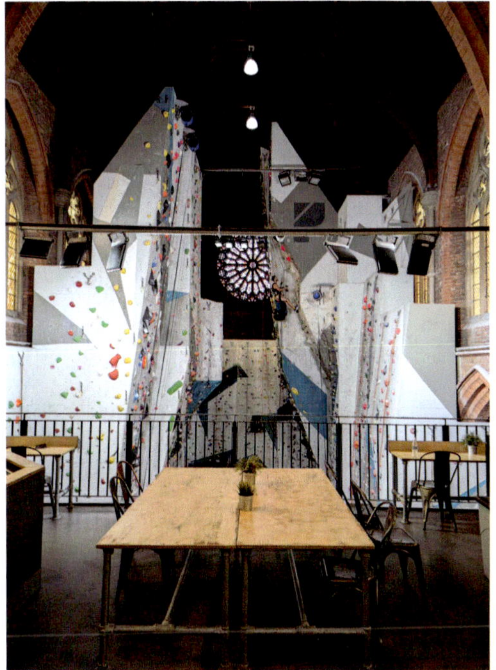

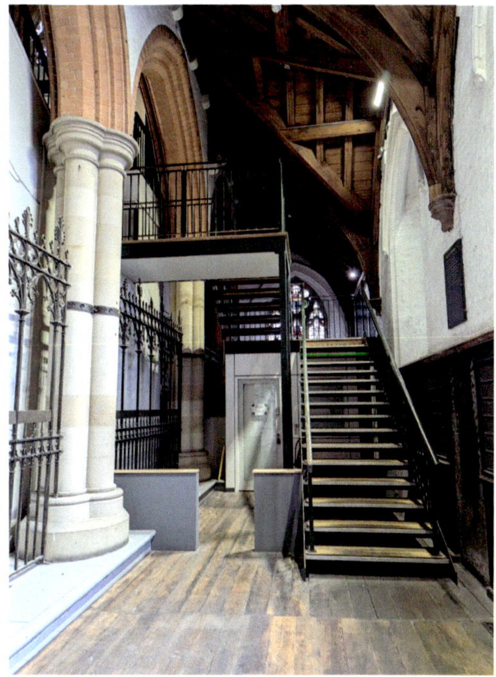

Above left: Interior of Church of St Benedict, Ardwick. Looking towards the interior west elevation.

Above right: Interior staircase, Church of St Benedict, Ardwick.

floor level and a chancel arch. Aisles present challenges, with many arched arcades separating them from another space. However, the challenge seems to have been overcome at Ardwick. Once inside, the standard terminology for the division of space in an ecclesiastical sense have been redefined to fit the new use. The former chancel is now the 'bouldering area' and the nave is the 'climbing area'. Metal staircases on either side of the former central worship space lead up to a large mezzanine floor with a retrofitted reception and café with seating overlooking the main climbing area. Climbing walls along the north and south nave aisles partially obscure a view of the aforementioned rose window, but several architectural features, fittings and furnishings can still be identified. A set of storage lockers are grouped beneath decorative iron parclose screens. An integral stone lectern is supported by a sculpture of an angel dating from *c.* 1900. The Historic England listing description states that this angel is life-sized, which is a misnomer; angels are incorporeal spirits and therefore not accurate indicators of measurement.

Some beautiful early twentieth-century stained glass remains in several of the windows visible in the modern building, and in spite of their elevation are in some cases accessible for closer inspection from the retrofitted staircases. There are some pleasant designs, mostly the work of T. F. Curtis, Ward and Hughes of London.

3. Ashton, St James

St James's Church on Cowhill Lane is thought to be the only church in Greater Manchester with two spires. It was designed by architect George Shaw of Uppermill under the instruction of a curate from Ashton-under-Lyne, Revd T. B. Dixon, who was tasked with forming a new parish for Ashton to provide a new church and school.

Construction was undertaken without delay between April and December in 1865. There is no doubt that the two spires are an unusual design feature of what is otherwise a modest and restrained Gothic Revival building, and the defining architectural feature of this local landmark. The spires projecting from the north and south-western corners of the nave, flank a fine five-light window with a wilted curvilinear tracery which is dulled by its external protective mesh covering. The west window, as viewed from Cowhill Lane, would be a more prominent feature if the ashlar stone dressings of the tracery and mullions were uncovered, matching the dressings of the towers, where almost all of the fabric is coarse rock-faced stone. Nevertheless, the elevation from Cowhill Lane is certainly striking.

The towers are square to their lowest stages, becoming octagonal with a gabled bell stage and stone spire above. Presumably there was a bell in each tower originally, or that was perhaps the intention, although the entry for St James's Church on the Dove's Guide for Bell Ringers online records only a single steel chime bell cast by Naylor, Vickers & Co. of Sheffield.

Once inside the building, it is clear that a reordering in more recent times has removed a large number of pews from the west end of the nave in order to provide sufficient meeting space with room for foldable tables and chairs as well as a basic servery. The remaining pews are utilitarian and not of great artistic

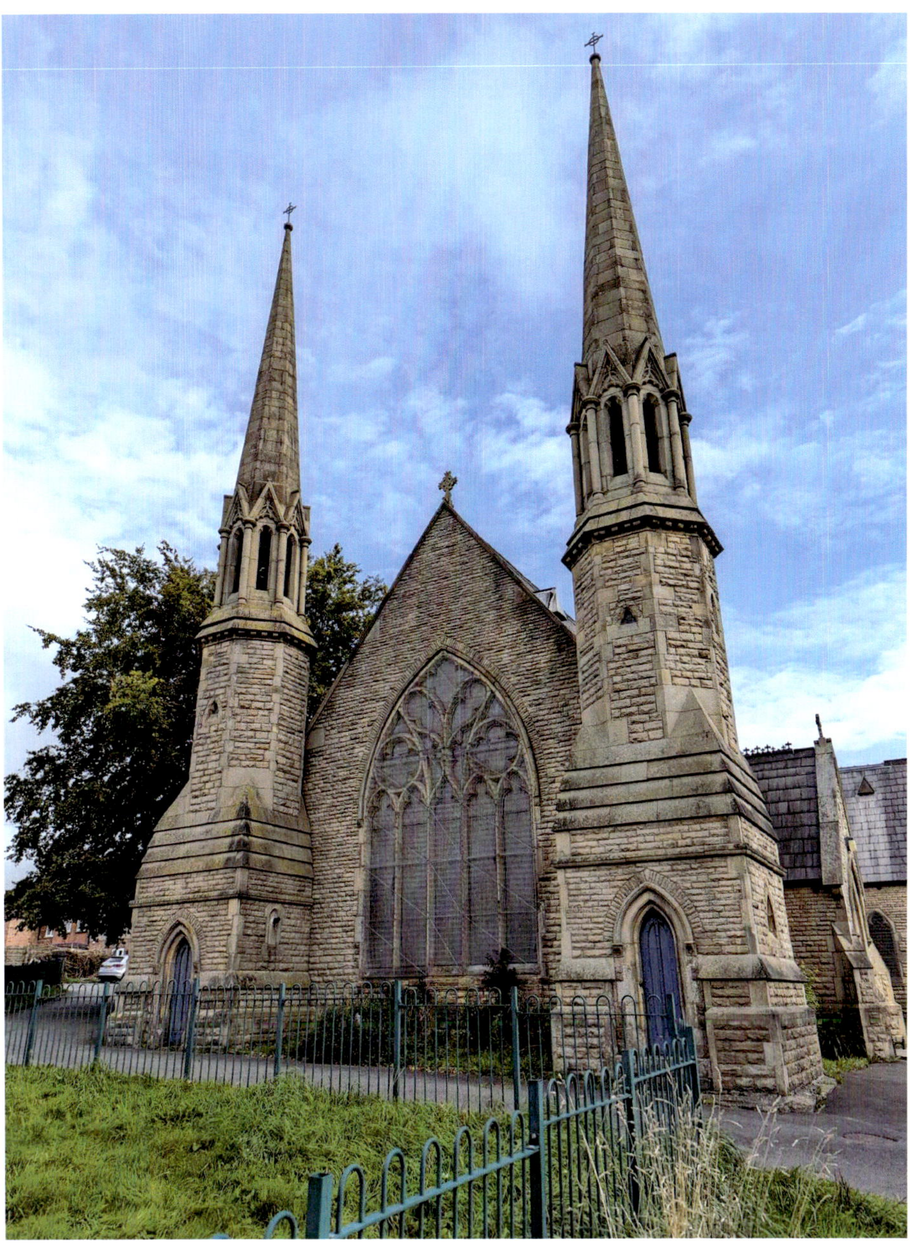

St James's, Ashton.

significance. These are located at the east end of the central worship space, in front of a broad dais and two wide transepts, leading to the chancel and its attractive three-light east window. The church was built originally to house 500 people, but its capacity was increased to accommodate 550 people after an expansion of the north transept.

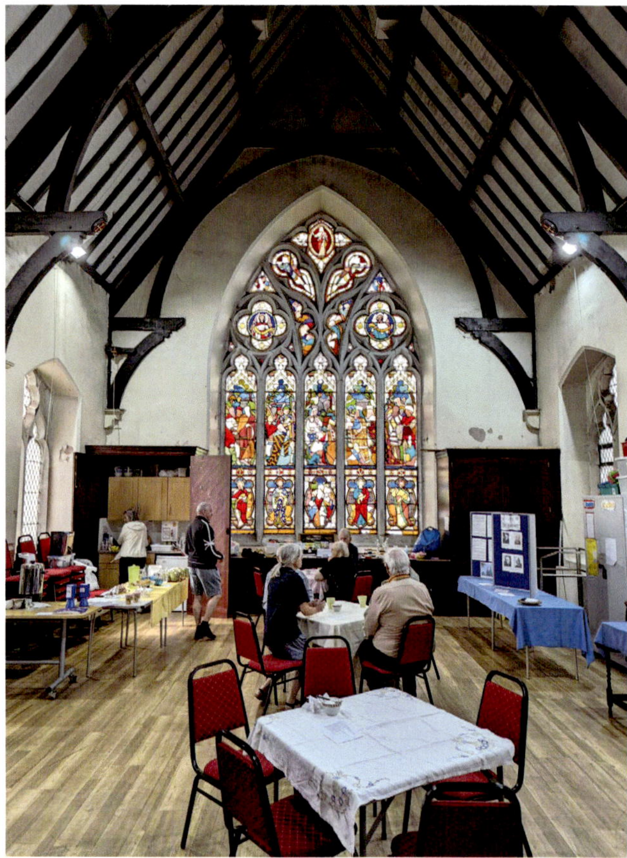

Interior of St James's,
looking west.

Each stained-glass window is worthy of closer inspection, especially the
St James window in the west wall of the north transept. This window was installed
in memory of Edwin Newton, who was the superintendent of Sunday schools
in Ashton. In February 1922, while out walking alone on Kinder Scout in the
Peak District, Edwin Newton slipped on ice and fell 50 feet over a cliff, fracturing
his skull. An unfortunate casualty of the interwar period boom in hiking. It is
reported that his body was not found for approximately fifteen days after his fall.

When I visited St James's Church in October 2023, the church was facing an
uncertain future as to whether it would remain open for worship or sadly have
to permanently close its doors after over 160 years of service. I attended a local
heritage open day arranged by the church, who had set out baptism and marriage
registers for inspection, along with photographs from years gone by of the
church, its congregation and clergy, as well as the local school and scout groups.
The remainder of 2023 was filled with concerts, coffee mornings and other events,
organised with the purpose of generating funds and local interest to keep the
church open and to demonstrate its value to the local community. The reader may
or may not find this church open in the future, but I hope they were successful in
their efforts at the time of writing.

4. ASHTON-UNDER-LYNE, ST MICHAEL AND ALL ANGELS

There is no other church in Greater Manchester I have wished to revisit so frequently as St Michael and All Angels' Church in Ashton-under-Lyne. That is to say that the splendour of its sensational interior is without equal in this area, which I will return to shortly. However, it is a large, imposing church and for several reasons is not easily appreciated when approached on foot from the town centre. Firstly, the A635 cuts horizontally straight across the path from the site of the old

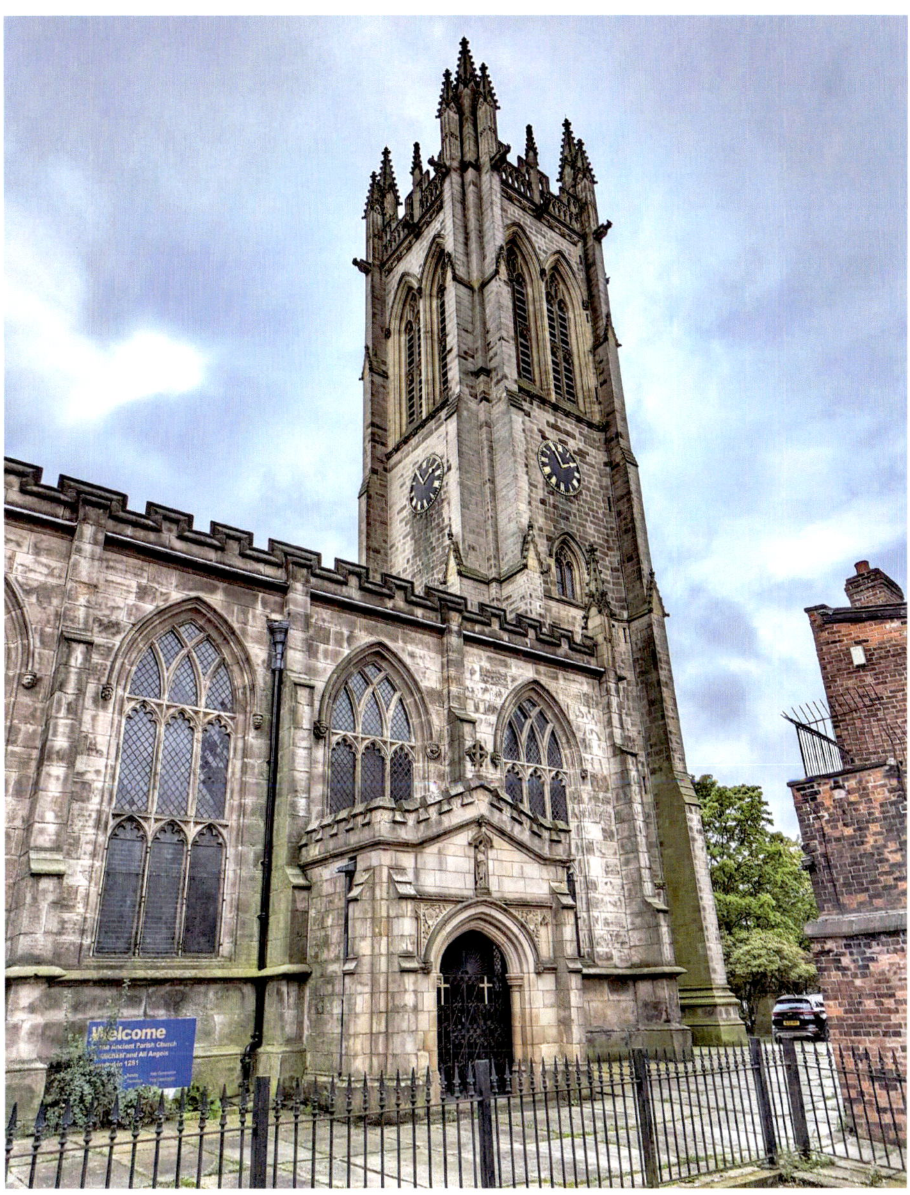

St Michael and All Angels, Ashton-under-Lyne.

manor house to the south. This path linked the ancient residence of the Assheton family to the private entrance of their chantry chapel at the east end of the church's south aisle, which later became the private family chapel of the earls of Stamford when the manor eventually passed to them in the eighteenth century. The A635 feeds into a ring road which also denies views of the east elevation of the church. Secondly, to the south and south-west of the building a substantial area of the churchyard is now a private car park. When Nikolaus Pevsner visited in 1968, the area now given over for car parking was still part of the churchyard and that aspect of the setting had not yet been disfigured. The view from Stamford Street to the north, partially masked by Victorian and later building is a little more in-keeping with the setting of the old town, but a view of any church's north elevation is rarely preferable (unless it has a feature of special architectural interest) than to those denied to us here by poorly considered twentieth-century intervention in its surroundings. As such, over half of the church cannot be fully appreciated from the town, and the church stands in a sort of 'dead end' overlooking main roads.

An earlier building on this site may be one of two recorded in the Domesday Book of 1086, and there was certainly a church here in 1262. Rebuilding commenced in the first half of the fifteenth century under the instruction of Sir John Assheton, who had acquired the advowson. It was Sir John's great-grandson, Sir Thomas Assheton, who left money for much of the surviving stained glass, recognised today to be of national significance, and also for the west tower. The original

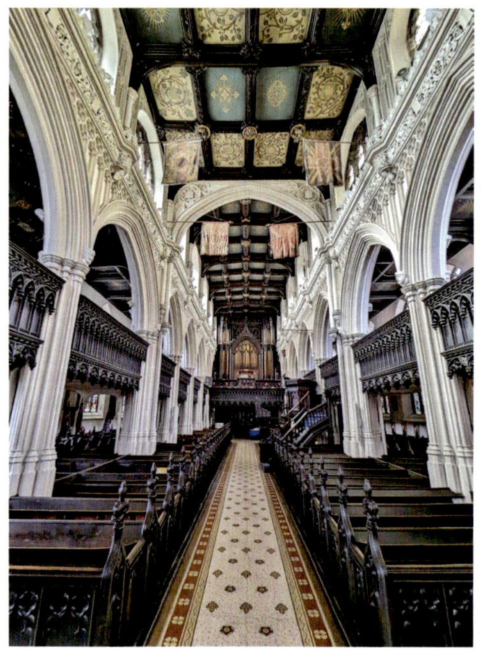

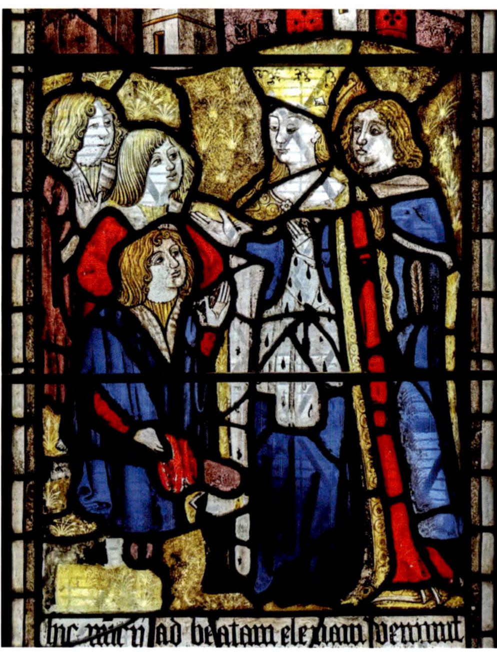

Above left: Interior of St Michael and All Angels, looking west.

Above right: Medieval stained glass depicting a scene from the life of St Helen, St Michael and All Angels Church.

tower was replaced by the one we see today by architect Joseph Stretch Crowter between 1886 and 1888, and it is not entirely dissimilar in appearance to that of Manchester Cathedral.

The treatment of the interior is nothing short of exquisite with its many gilded, moulded and decorated surfaces. A little time should be spent first wandering up and down the aisles at your own pace simply observing this complex building and absorbing as much information as possible. It is elaborate but not fussy. It is not clear how much of the existing fabric is late medieval in date, purportedly concealed beneath a bold scheme of panelling and frieze work facing the nave arcades, or how strictly what we see today follows the decoration of an earlier scheme. The medieval ceiling is masked by later plasterwork, added when a major reordering was undertaken at the end of the eighteenth century, which follows the form if not the detail of the original. No compromise has been made on the decorative scheme and much of it is architectural rather than artistic. This was implemented at the same time that the church was re-pewed and the old screen and rood removed, although the plan of furnishings and fittings was again overhauled in the mid-nineteenth century.

The existing furnishings represent a sequence of rare completeness of the 1840s comparable only with Leeds Minster, formerly the parish church dedicated to St Peter in Leeds (West Yorkshire). The architectural setting was influenced by the Oxford movement to enable Anglicanism to move towards a 'high-church' style of worship which was reflected in a better understanding of Gothic architecture. The result at Ashton-under-Lyne has undergone some alteration and is therefore a little more

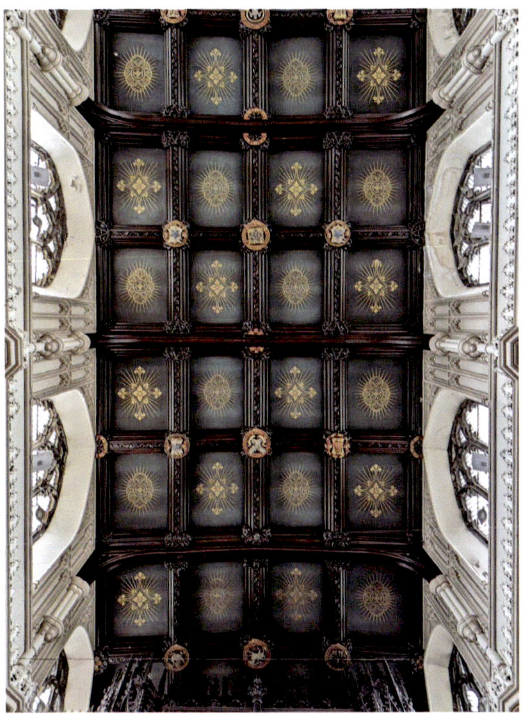

Nave ceiling, St Michael and All Angels, Ashton-under-Lyne.

conventional compared to Leeds Minster as set out by architect Robert D. Chantrell, with Ashton-under-Lyne eventually having a distinct chancel, refitted by Crowther between 1881 and 1889. The character of an auditory worship space remains, fitted with box pews (some of which face with their backs to the chancel), a three-decker pulpit placed against a north nave arcade and spacious galleries.

The medieval stained glass has been described as the best preserved and most significant in the north-west of England. It is the most ambitious surviving St Helen cycle surviving in English late medieval art, given to the church in *c.* 1497–1512 by Sir Thomas Assheton. As the reader navigates the various windows where late medieval glass has been reset, it must be remembered that some of the scenes are out of sequence, but there are several handy guides available in the church to establish the correct order in which the scenes can be followed. Much of the glass was originally in the great east window before it was removed to its present location in 1872. The glazing was sensitively cleaned and conserved in the twentieth century, and it is to those specialist glaziers we must be grateful for such careful reconstruction and restoration. It is not often that such complete schemes of late medieval stained glass from this period can be seen at eye level and in person. A total of twenty scenes depict the life of St Helen, with members of the Assheton family represented as donor figures to the benefaction and embellishment of the church, knelt in prayer in the bottom of the lower panels, including Sir Thomas Assheton himself with his two wives.

5. Bolton, All Souls

A fine example of vertically pronounced Victorian Perpendicular Gothic in beautiful brick, All Souls' is a masterpiece by Lancashire architects Edward Paley and Hubert Austin, built for the Greenhouse brothers, local mill owners, and dates from 1881. Crompton is a suburb of red-brick terraces and large industrial buildings. All Souls' Church is no different and draws directly from the local tradition; a beacon in brick, standing well above the lower terraces with a stamp of authority. On occasion, the Victorians could be quite fussy about carved brick ornamentation, adorning the façades of their grand buildings, but in this case, Paley and Austin limited the ornamentation of All Souls' Church to chequerboard brickwork and otherwise let the combination of stone dressings stand out against the brick. The church was built at a time when the standard of brick manufacture in England had improved considerably. Through the use of clay being pressed in moulds and advances in commercial kiln engineering, it had become possible several decades earlier to produce bricks that were consistent in colour, texture and most importantly in size. As such, the texture and colour of the building fabric of All Souls' Church is so precise that it appears altogether quite pristine in finish and without defects.

After standing empty and derelict for nearly two decades and being considered by some locals as a bit of an eyesore, the church reopened in 2014 after a £4.9 million restoration and regeneration project funded by the Heritage Lottery Fund, with support from the Churches Conservation Trust and local campaign leader and champion of the community Inayat Omarji MBE. The project

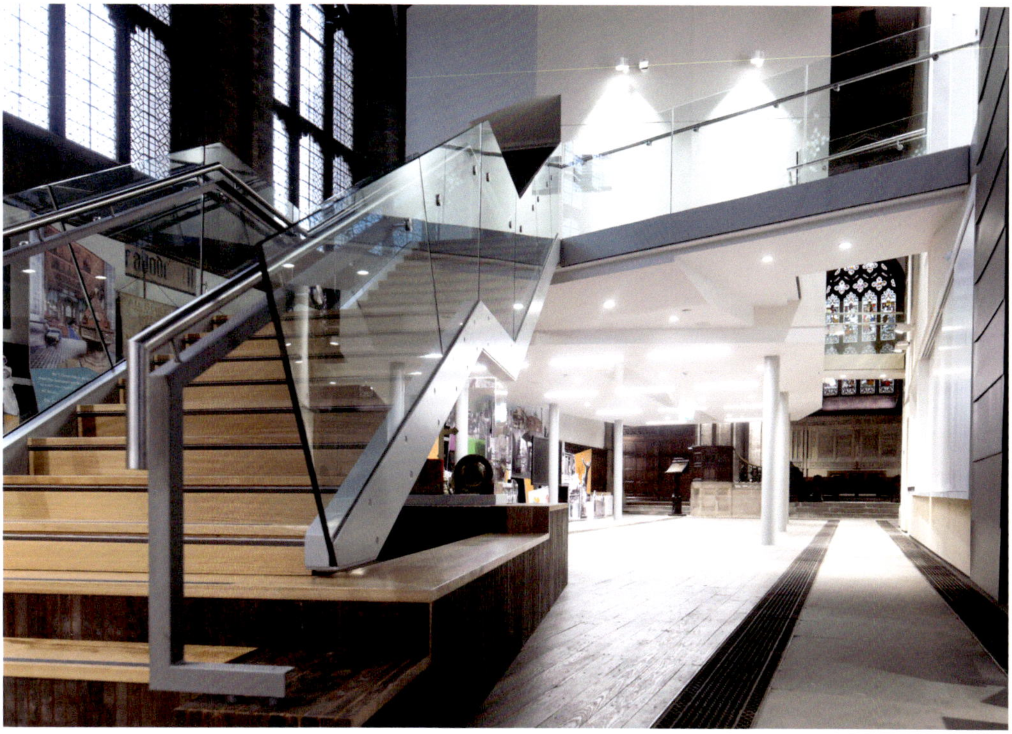

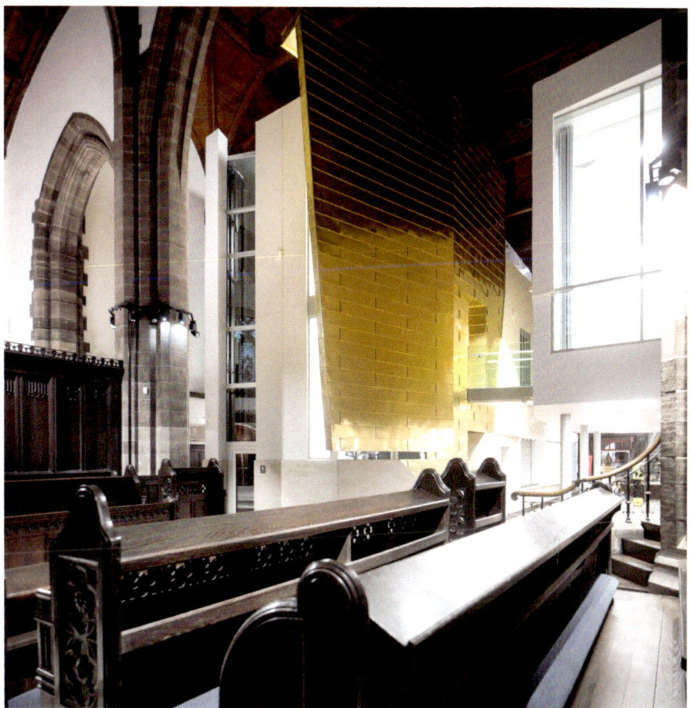

Above and right:
All Souls' Church,
Bolton. (Courtesy of
Andy Marshall)

to revive the building had been in action since 2007 and was special in that it provided a unique opportunity for several young trainee tradespeople on work placements to get involved in the restoration of various parts of the building – from stonemasonry to carpentry – in restoring the roofs and glazing, all to further their own knowledge and experience in working on a listed heritage building. After much hard work to restore the fabric of the building and make it safe for occupation, innovative interior pods were installed providing a unique meeting space whilst leaving the historic fabric largely untouched. This created much needed office and social space for local businesses and the wider community which are today tenanted out. All Souls' Church now has a new lease of life and has once again become a valued community asset, revived so as to stay relevant to its community. Once more it serves as a vibrant part of the local cultural landscape.

6. BURNAGE, ST NICHOLAS

St Nicholas's Church is perhaps Greater Manchester's most significant Anglican church of the interwar period and sits heavily set back from the Kingsway in its suburban setting south of Manchester. This sheer, yellowish-grey brick-faced building, not dissimilar to his slightly later apsed church dedicated to the Epiphany in Gipton (Leeds, West Yorkshire), was built between 1930 and 1932. Driving

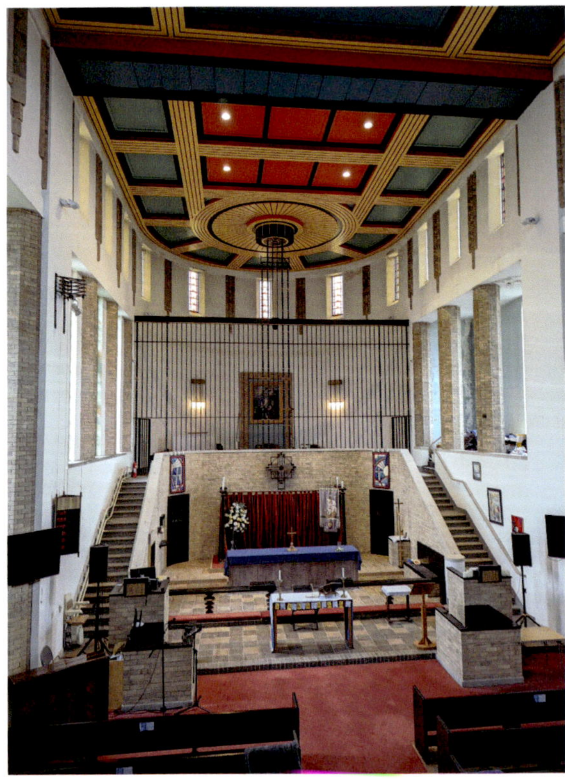

St Nicholas Church, Burnage.
Interior looking east.

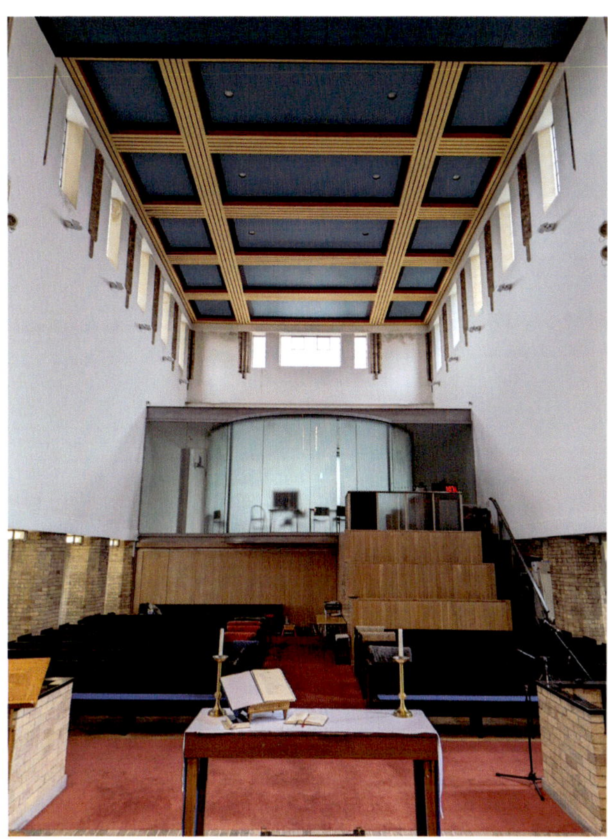

St Nicholas Church,
Burnage. Interior
looking west.

along the Kingsway in Burnage, one would be forgiven for at a glance mistaking this style of architecture for that adapted by Odeon cinemas of the same period.

St Nicholas's was the first of two large churches in Manchester designed by Nugent Cachemaille-Day of Welch, Cachemaille-Day and Lander architects, Lincoln's Inn in London. St Nicholas's Church is not surpassed in merit by his later church dedicated to All Angels at Lawton Moor in Northenden, although it predates it and is given full attention in this book because it represents 'a milestone in the history of church architecture in England' as noted by art historian Nikolaus Pevsner. An extension of approximately 25 feet was added to the west end of the church in 1964 by Cachemaille-Day, almost thirty years after it was originally built to his own designs. He is purported to have liked the fact that St Nicholas's Church was both his first job and last, bookending a long career in architecture.

It was anticipated from its conception that noise from traffic on the busy Kingsway (A34) would potentially interrupt services, so to combat this problem Cachemaille-Day proposed to locate the vestries and offices on the ground floor of the western apse, behind the high altar with the Lady Chapel on top, accessed by two staircases from the nave. Moving the high altar forward in this way created a sense of space and emphasised the perpendicular qualities of the thin, high windows and buff brick columns of the first-floor chancel aisle arcades.

There are several other original features worthy of note. Of particular interest for those with a penchant for the more practical and everyday church fittings is the hymn indicator, which is of emerging modernist design with stylised red lettering against a curved black and gold board. The small south transept houses extraordinarily large, telescopic cover over a stone font. Painted to match the nave ceiling in gold, blue and red.

I have undertaken a fuller assessment of this church because it has been quite substantially altered and reordered within the past two decades. The church was rededicated by the Bishop of Manchester on 23 June 2002, in between extensive works carried out from 2001 to 2003 by architect Anthony Grimshaw of Wigan, who also undertook work to restore the exterior fabric in 2016. The footprint of this spacious twentieth-century building lent itself well to adaptation and the resulting divisions of the lofty interior appear to make obvious sense. Grimshaw's reordering transformed the west end of the central worship space so that it was converted into a hall for community use. This was achieved by inserting a retractable screen between the new hall and the nave. However, it was the installation of a striking glass meeting room at first-floor level above the new partitioned screen which was most ambitious and completed to great effect, adjacent with the elevated Lady Chapel. It does not detract from the character of the interior setting and the internal view towards the apsed chancel is not spoiled, with rising steps to a screened-off Lady Chapel above the high altar. A reordering on this scale required an improved heating system and underfloor heating were also installed in 2002.

For readers interested in inspecting original plans of what the church looked like prior to its reordering, you will find mounted on a wall in a south corridor a framed copy of original working drawings and plans dated May 1931 drafted by Cachemaille-Day.

7. BURY, ST MARY

St Mary's Church was a medieval landmark in the centre of Bury. Up until 1842 when the church had a late medieval west tower attached to a wide Georgian nave, the latter built in a fairly ubiquitous classical style. The tower was rebuilt in 1842 and 1843 by Adolphus Henry Cates, a York-based architect whose full career and list of works are little known today. Cates is believed to be the architect who designed the simple Gothic Revival church dedicated to St Andrew in Great Fencote (North Yorkshire), which closed for worship in 2019, and several cemetery headstones across Yorkshire.

Cates's mid-century west tower and steeple remain today along with a group of earlier monuments mounted high on the walls in the base of the tower, but the rest of the church was rebuilt by Joseph Stretch Crowther between 1871 and 1876. Looking upwards and eastwards inside Crowther's church, the brick-lined walls and stone-dressed nave arcades are very pleasing on the eye and it is an overall well-considered design. Unusually, although not entirely uncommon for a large town parish church, there is a nave clerestory with an internal walkway which must give a spectacular view of the deep hammerbeam roof structure above.

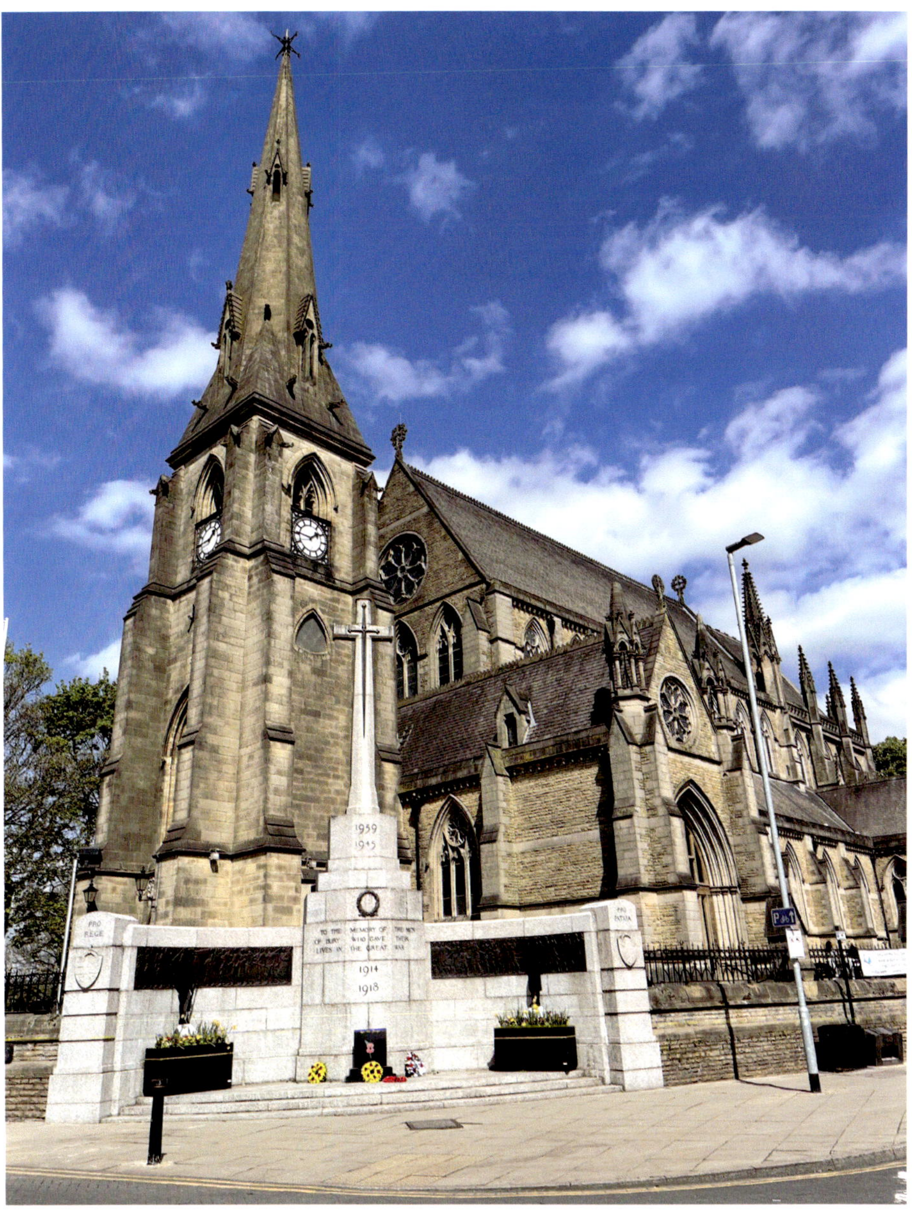

St Mary's, Bury. (Courtesy of Lucilla Gray)

Standing at the west end of the church with your back to the modern timber and glass partition screen separating the narthex from the nave, all eyes are drawn along a path of Minton tiles towards the chancel. Here, behind an intricate wrought-iron screen is a series of remarkable paintings made on copper sheets, mounted inside the moulded arches of blind arcading sweeping circling the walls of the apsidal east end surrounding the high altar. They depict St Mary, Mother of Christ, in various

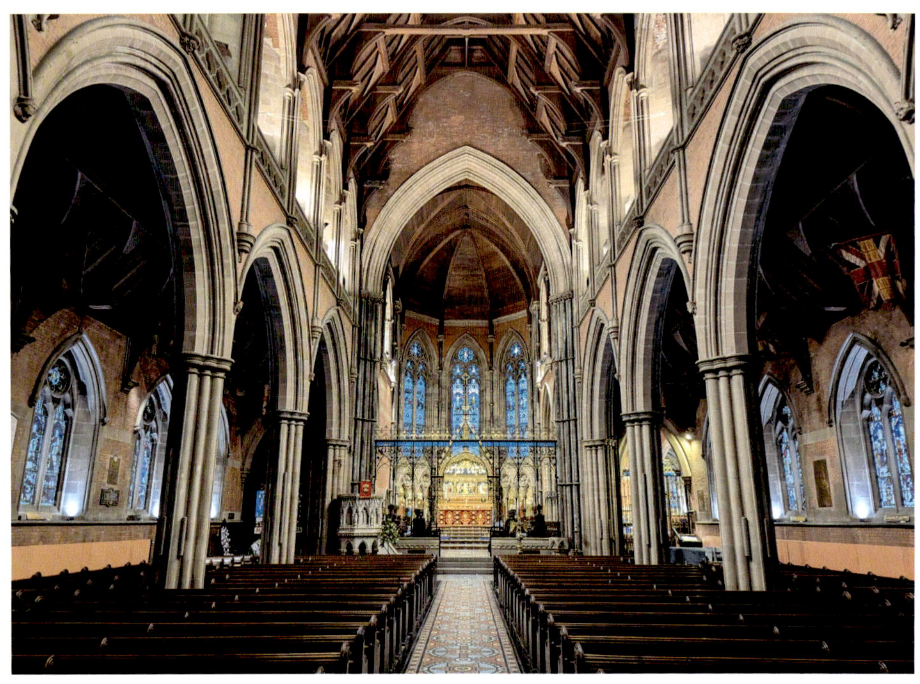

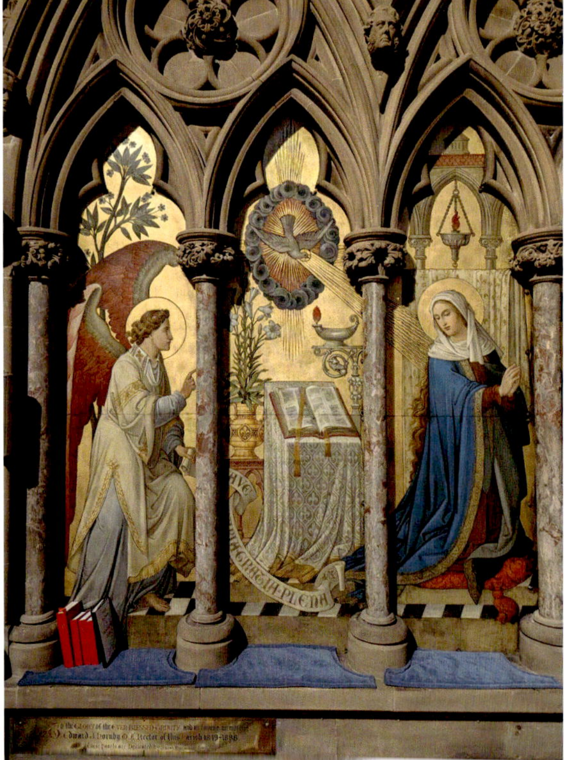

Above: Interior of St Mary's, looking east.

Left: Chancel painting of the Annunciation on copper sheets, St Mary's Bury.

scenes including the Annunciation with the visitation of the Archangel Gabriel, the birth of Christ and the visitation of the Three Magi. What is also impressive about these panels is how the artist had clearly considered the setting in which they would be installed and has cleverly incorporated the stonework of the blind arcading as an architectural setting for each scene. The paintings were donated in *c.* 1880 and appear to be in remarkable condition. The copper background of each sheet has a warm glow in the downlit setting of the apsidal chancel. The opulent decoration in the chancel is in fact all part of one holistic scheme, including the stained glass, most of which is by Hardman & Co., and a painted reredos by J. Harold Gibbons.

8. CHADDERTON, ST MARK

Chadderton is a suburbanised and post-industrial settlement of which modern expansion has over time connected it to the town of Oldham, a mile to the west. Before the cotton mills came to Chadderton, the town was largely dispersed around agricultural land and pasture at the foothills of the Pennines. Today, the town is relatively ordinary in and of itself, with reasonable access to some of the area's finest historic churches.

Several churches were built in Chadderton following the New Parishes Act of 1844. The last church to be built in 1960 was the parish church dedicated to St Mark, designed entirely by York-based ecclesiastical architect George G. Pace. Construction was complete by 1963 and the church was listed Grade II in September 1998. Nikolaus Pevsner wrote in 1969: 'One must leave it to Mr Pace – he is always fresh and never afraid to experiment, and he does not follow all the latest fashions.' The updated volume of *The Buildings of England* for this area states that this freshness has not been lost. I would agree that twenty years on from that brief assessment, the same can generally be said again.

At the height of his career Pace was engaged in churning out designs for many new church buildings (and their ancillary rooms) and furnishings. His thoughtful and meticulous approach meant that progress was generally slow, with some projects spanning decades from start to finish. St Mark's Church was the exception and was completed in three years, which is half the time it took to complete his contemporary church in Wythenshawe.

I met the present incumbent of St Mark's Church, Father Stephen Smith, for a short tour of the building. This modernist church is a mix of sharp geometry and straight, hard lines, but it is starting to show its age. It was reassuring to hear that steps have been made to keep on top of regular maintenance. Secondary glazing over the gridded windows has been installed in isolated areas and fundraising for roof works to the Lady Chapel are ongoing (part of a larger project which has seen the impressive saddleback tower roof already renewed).

The interior of the main worship space is of white brick, exposed concrete beams and stone paving. Architecturally, the construction of the pitched ceiling is remarkable in its design, supported by Y-shaped supports and complemented neatly by suspended wooden lantern-shape light fittings. As one might expect with Pace, the plan of a wide and lofty nave is extended through a series of ancillary parish rooms, which conceal an irregular overall footprint.

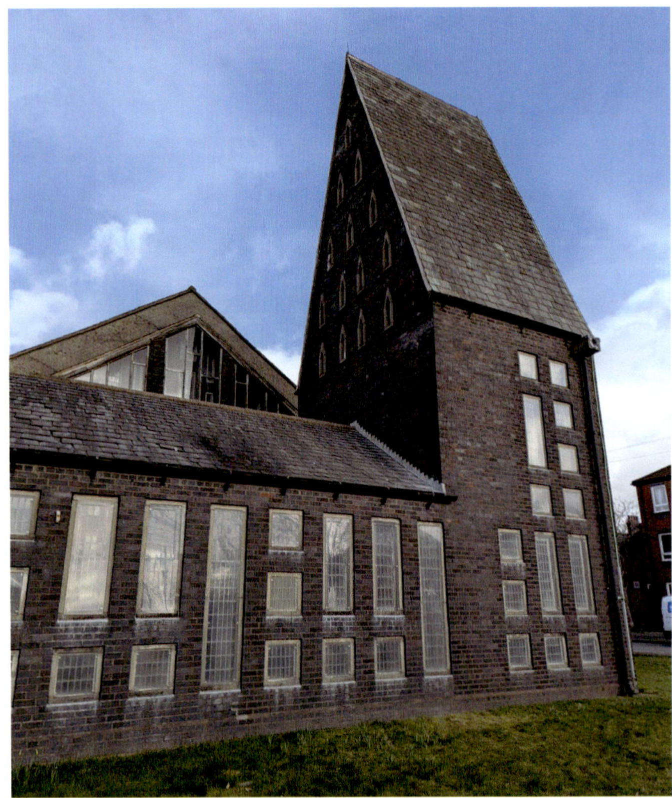

Left: St Mark's, Chadderton.

Below left: Interior of St Mark's, looking east.

Below right: Font and font cover, St Mark's, Chadderton.

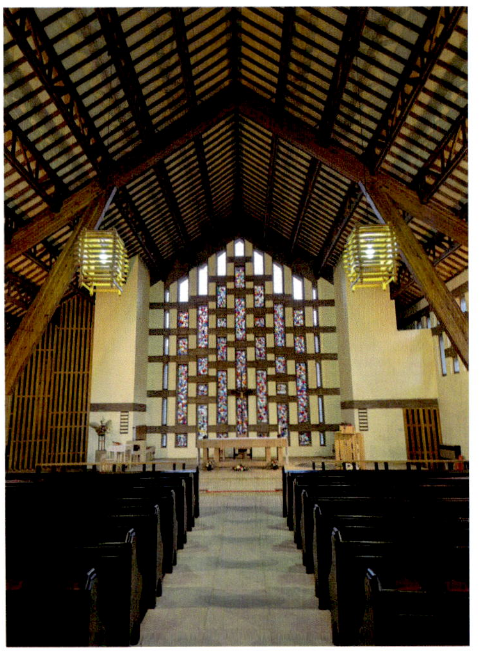

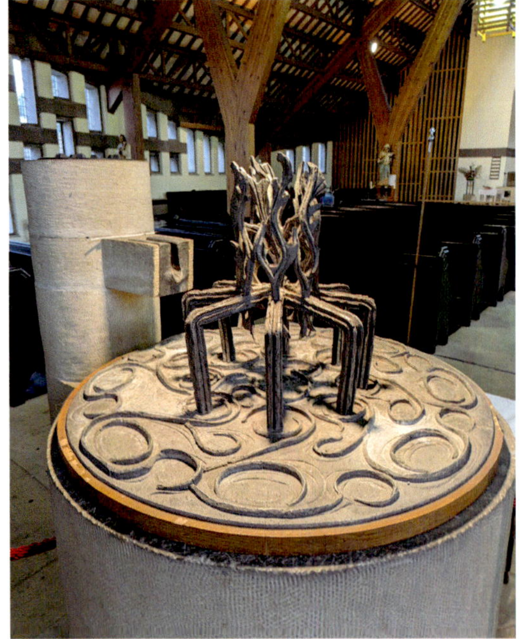

Yet there is a restrained character to the arrangement of furnishings and fittings in the central worship space, and one wonders if the scheme could have been more ambitious. The pews are reclaimed from another church, perhaps to save costs. Pews or benches of his own design (and a great many survive in other churches and chapels) would certainly feel more compatible here. Everything else is of wrought iron and English oak. Special attention should be given to the baptismal font in the central worship space, which is nothing short of a work of art. Perhaps it was a collaboration between Pace and Frank Roper, a sculptor and glazier who is known to have worked on occasion with Pace for his new churches. The design of the sculptural font cover is characteristic of Roper's work. It depicts the Holy Spirit and swirling water, symbolic of being immersed in or filled with the Holy Spirit.

The only coloured glazing is in the east window. The largest of the gridded windows, it incorporates fragments of nineteenth-century stained and painted glass (some of it in imitation of fifteenth-century stained glass), purportedly removed from demolished churches in the local area, of which there were numerous in the previous century so this is not an unreasonable assumption. Pace undoubtedly had access to recycled material. This is a charming modernist church, sitting quietly amongst residential development on the Middleton Road to Oldham. It is not given enough attention compared to the architect's more renowned church in Wythenshawe, of which Pevsner described as almost as raw and wide as Chadderton.

9. CHEADLE, ST MARY

Looking across the high street towards the south elevation of St Mary's Parish Church, with the handsome White Hart pub to the left, it is hard to imagine that in 1523 this fine sandstone church was reported to be 'in great ruin and decay'. The building we see today would be unrecognisable only a few decades later as it was promptly and almost entirely rebuilt by the mid-sixteenth century. This act of renewal of the parish church was due to the generous benefaction and embellishment of local gentry, who bequeathed large sums of money to the church authorities for its rebuilding, which resulted in private chantry chapels being added to the east ends of the north and south aisles at the same time. These structures survive to this day along with some contemporary woodwork of the highest quality, screening them from the rest of the interior worship space. These are the Brereton and Savage chapels, delineated by oak screens with sumptuous carvings. This is a church with much ancient timber, all quite darkly stained and eye-catching. The wooden screen around the Savage Chapel contains an inscription which reads: 'Pray for the souls of John Savage 'militis' and Elizabeth his wife, their songs and daughters who caused this chapel to be in the year of the delivery of the Virgin 1529.'

The Brereton Chapel in the adjacent south aisle is contemporary with the Savage Chapel but has a much finer carved wooden screen, dividing it off on two sides from the rest of the nave. The panels on one side are carved with a standard Tudor linenfold pattern, but as you work your way up the screen, the detail really comes to life. Horizontal wooden panels are pierced through with repeated Gothic forms such as mouchettes, quatrefoils and daggers, and there is almost as much pierced

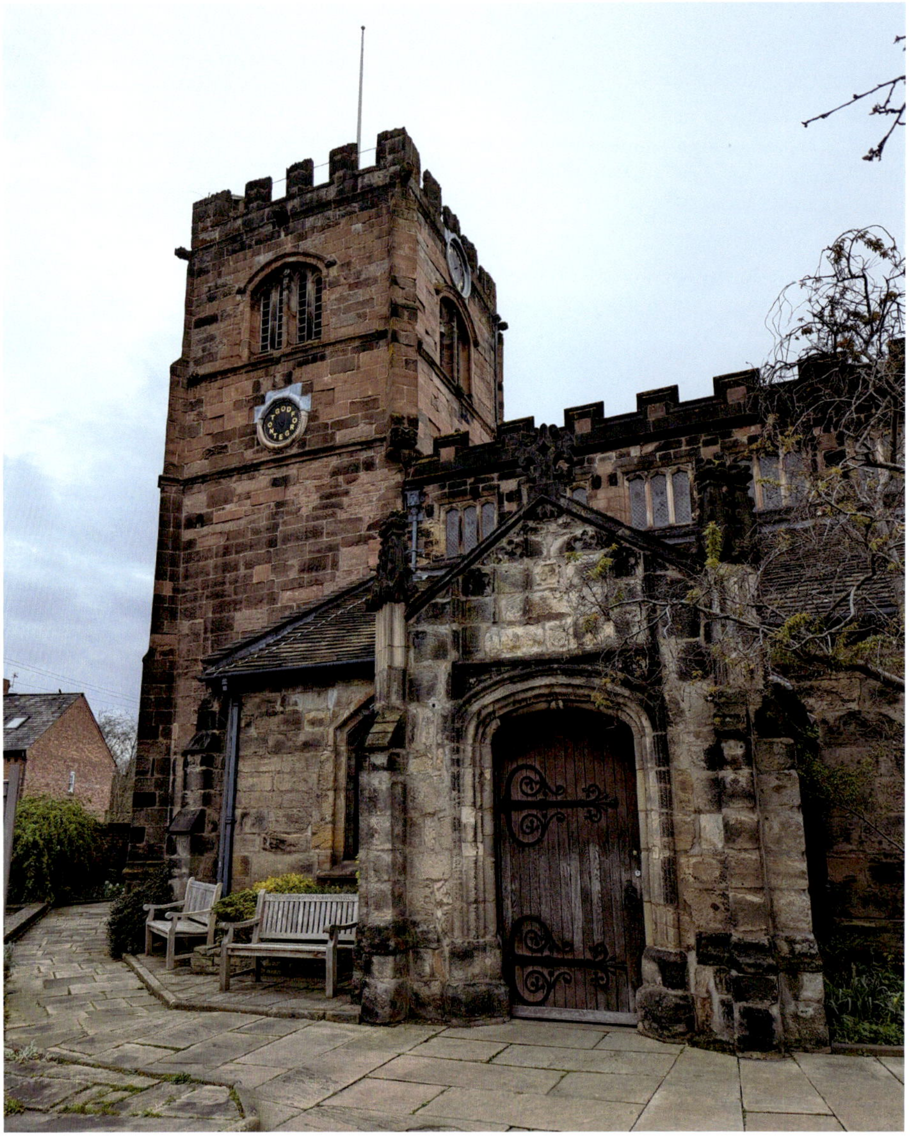

St Mary's, Cheadle.

space as there is solid wood. Mouldings in one section are decorated with carved 'tuns' or wine barrels, purported to be a play on the Brere-*ton* name. The Brereton Chapel has three effigial monuments and although they commemorate members of the same family, they are clearly different in costume and date. The first is a chest tomb with two alabaster knights dating to roughly 1460 and it is important to remember that these are older than this church itself by several decades. There is also a stone recumbent effigy of Sir Thomas Brereton of Handforth, who died in 1673, on a tomb chest with shields. Of the three effigies, the latter has not fared

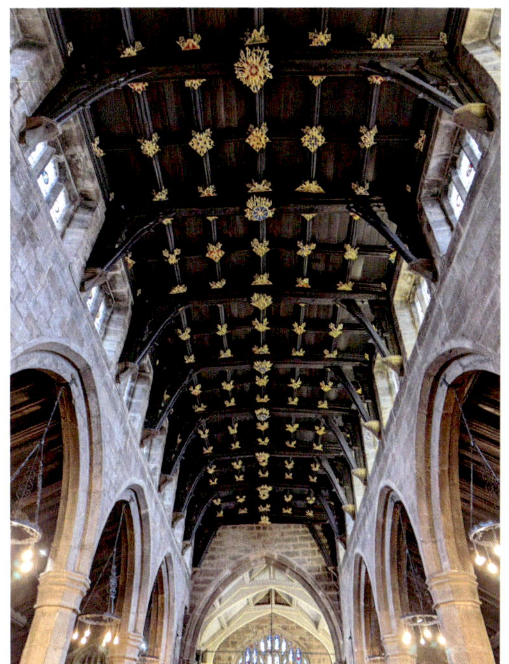

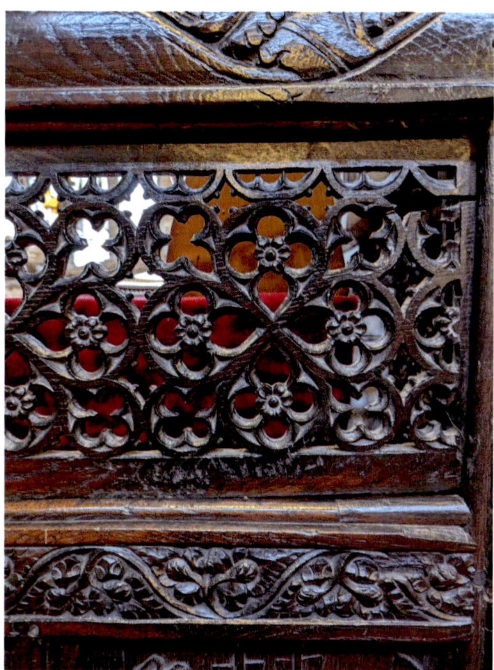

Above left: Nave ceiling looking east, St Mary's, Cheadle.

Above right: Detail of medieval parclose screen, St Mary's, Cheadle.

Right: North aisle and pre-Conquest cross fragment in a display case, St Mary's, Cheadle.

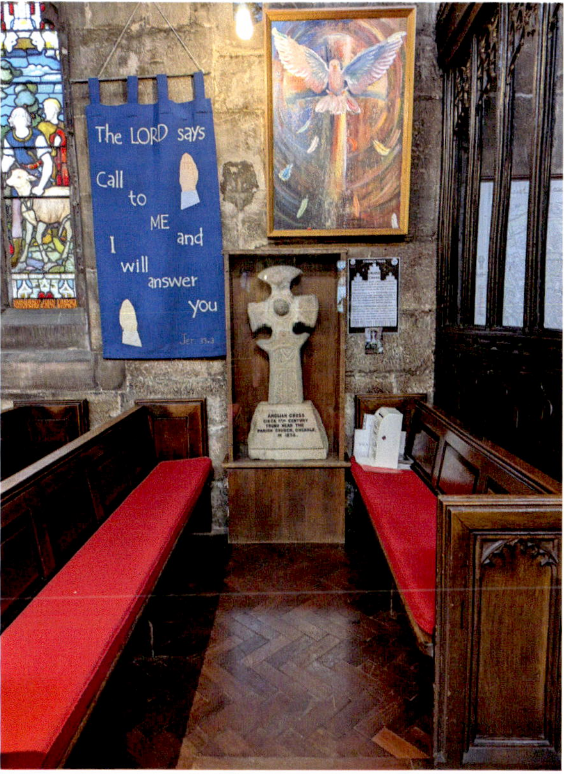

the best. Sir Thomas has lost his hands, as is not uncommon, and although his ancestors carved in alabaster are well worn, they have survived remarkably well.

In the north aisle is a fragment of a pre-Conquest standing stone cross. A rarity in Greater Manchester. It is formed of a cross head and decorated shaft and is understood to date from the eleventh century. The cross fragment was discovered near the church in 1874 and is displayed in a typically antiquarian manner in its own special case with an inscribed plinth. This has been interpreted by some to mean there was Christian settlement and activity nearby from an early date in the locality, but it alone does not confirm with absolute certainty the presence of an early church on this site.

The nave was overhauled during the rigorous and thorough rebuild of the sixteenth century, and the ceiling above it is a master construction of braced oak beams and brightly gilded ceiling bosses. Special attention should also be paid to the scars on the solid walls of the north and south nave arcade, along the line of the current chancel screen. Where the staircase which once led from the ground floor opens out at the top of the site of the former medieval rood screen, indents can be seen in the stone of the platform level and front balustrade, possibly indicating the presence of a once substantial screen.

This and so much more survived a major restoration in 1875 and the reordering of 1991. The present custodians and churchwardens of St Mary's have greatly enriched the experience of visiting this ancient church and have taken great care to preserve the items of historical and artistic interest, whilst adapting the space for their current needs. I was delighted to hear of regular open days and an extensive on-site archive of churchyard burial plans, each headstone and plot hand illustrated and numbered into the hundreds.

10. DEANE, ST MARY

Within the curtilage of this large churchyard an ancient church is nestled, held secret and set back from the comings and goings of modern Greater Manchester. Formerly a chapel of ease in the parish of Eccles until it was made parochial in its own right in the sixteenth century, 'Saynte Mariden's' Chapel, now St Mary's Church, is the most rural of ancient churches on the outskirts of Bolton. Of course, it is not at all rural nowadays, but once very much was, occupying a site within an extensive wooded churchyard which rolled downhill to the Middlebrook. Set well back from the busy Wigan Road, the church takes its name from the narrow, wooded dean – Deane Clough – to the west of the building. Most of the present fabric dates from the sixteenth century and only the tower is slightly older with a reset thirteenth-century door. Sadly, the tower has lost the little spire it once had, although this survives in pictorial evidence through antiquarian drawings.

The church is low and long with an unusual arrangement of different types of window when viewed from the south. Both the embattled south aisle and nave have numerous square-headed windows of three or four lights, some of which have evidently been renewed with cleaner stone, yet to darken with age. The nave clerestory was added in 1833 and is in-keeping with the earlier fabric of the building, although surely the need couldn't have been for more natural light

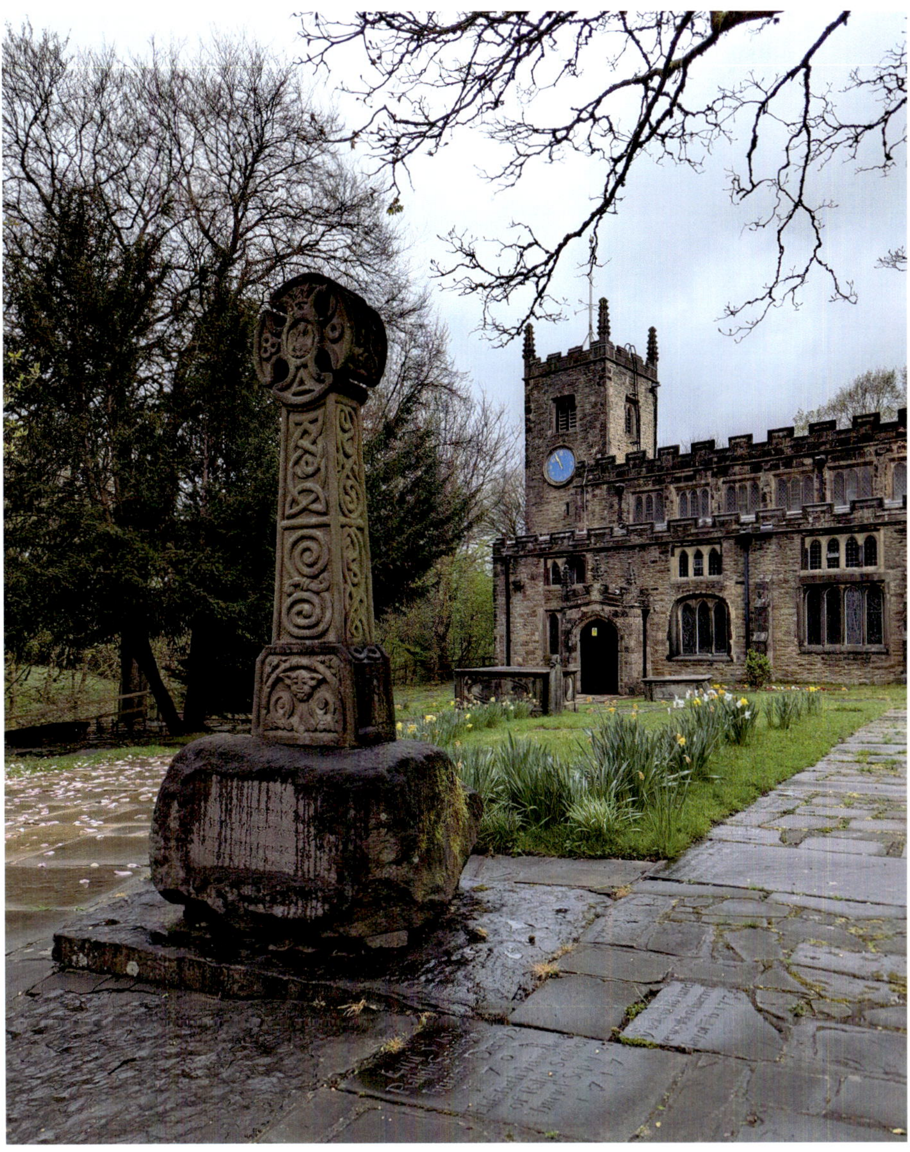

Nineteenth-century memorial cross to the memory of the martyr George Marsh at St Mary's, Deane.

unless to provide greater visibility for the internal seating galleries which has now been removed. The fenestration of the chancel is an unexpected and rather heavy-handed expression of Victorian Perpendicular, probably the result of a major restoration and refurbishment in the time of Revd Henry Sheridan Patterson, after which the church reopened for worship in December 1884.

Looking east down the nave's central aisle, there is an unobstructed line of sight down to the great east window. Until the mid-nineteenth century when

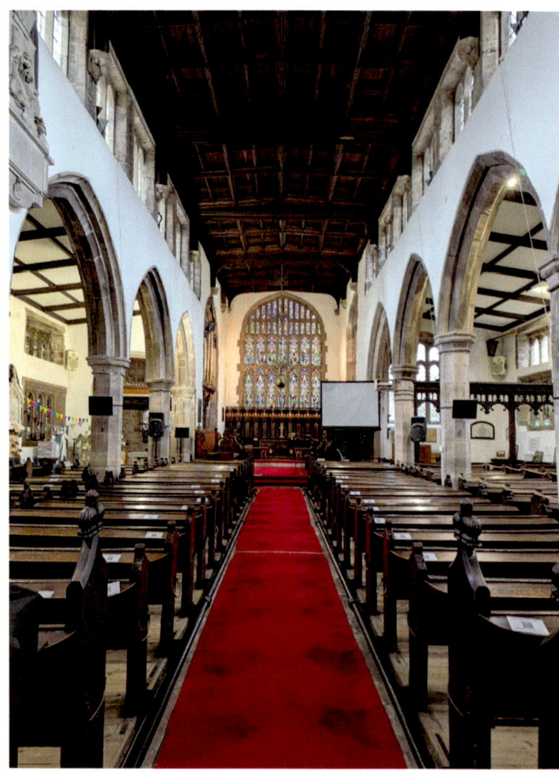

Left: Interior looking east, St Mary's, Deane.

Below left: Detail of altar panel depicting the martyrdom of George Marsh, St Mary's, Deane.

Below right: Pew end detail with acorn design, St Mary's, Deane.

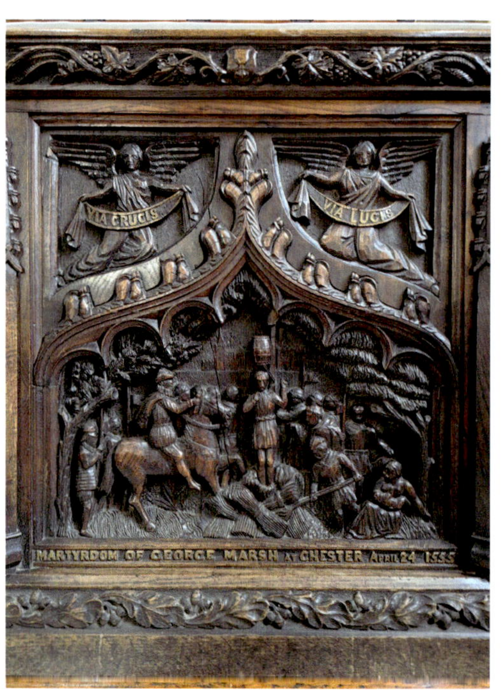

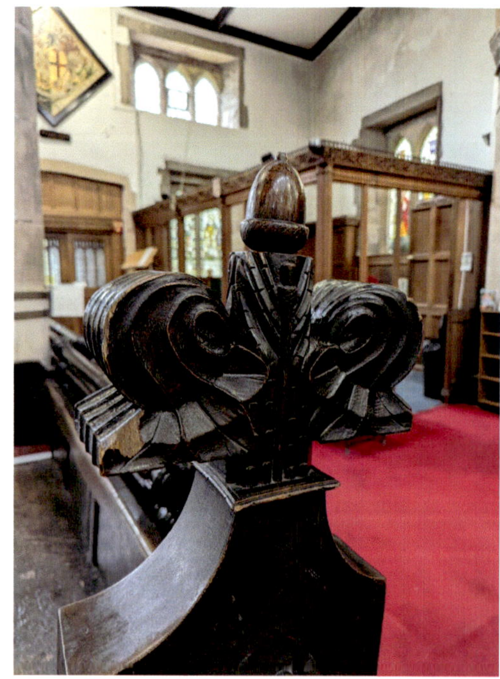

the church was heavily pewed and with internal galleries, a large seventeenth-century pulpit known as 'the Martyrs Pulpit' was installed centrally so that all seats were orientated to hear the spoken word of the minister. Pictorial evidence shows that the pulpit was supported by a rail that joined it to the reading or clerk's desk. The pulpit still survives but it has been displaced to one side of the church, and thankfully not entirely mutilated. The pews and choir stalls are all probably early nineteenth century in date, some with 'poppy heads' and clunky, vernacular-style oaks with acorns. In the chancel, the ornate front panelling of the high altar has a central low relief panel depicting the martyrdom of George Marsh, burned at Chester on 24 April 1555 because 'he was true to his conscience and to the faith of Christ', like so many who met their end during that time of Protestant persecution. Marsh was a resident of Deane and is included in *Foxe's Book of Martyrs*, published in 1563. A nineteenth-century memorial window also commemorates Marsh, but it is the churchyard memorial cross to the local martyr which most visitors will notice upon first entering and leaving the churchyard from the south. This separately listed Grade II monument is an unassuming Celtic-style stone cross, carved in relief upon its rough surface with patterns and beasts of pre-Conquest influence. It bears an inscription which records that 'this stone formerly stood on New York Road, Deane, and was removed to this site by the inhabitants of Deane, 1893', erected by Revd Henry Sheridan Patterson.

11. DENTON, ST ANNE (HAUGHTON)

St Anne's Church is an extraordinary Arts and Crafts building by architect brothers James Medland Taylor and Henry Taylor, built between 1880 and 1882. At one time in their career they shared an office in St Ann's Square in central Manchester. St Anne's Church is located no less than 6 miles from Manchester city centre and was built for its patron Edward Joseph Sidebotham, a local industrialist and chemist with an interest in botany, in memory of his late wife. The building is quite extraordinary in terms of its sheer size and many vernacular and ornate details. It sits within a pleasant landscaped churchyard full of trees. Unfortunately, visitors in recent years may not have seen the interior as Historic England added St Anne's Church to the Heritage at Risk Register in April 2022 following concerns about ground settlement around the font and nave as a result of vibrations from the nearby M67 motorway. Remedial works were completed in 2024 with financial support from National Highways and Historic England, after which the church was removed from the Heritage at Risk register. Although at the time of writing engineering and construction work to the nearby M67 remains ongoing and access to the churchyard is sadly restricted.

Arts and Crafts churches are important because they represent a unique fusion of artistic expression, craftsmanship and spirituality. St Anne's overall attractiveness is probably best appreciated on inspection from the south corner of the churchyard by the lychgate, where its romantic architectural qualities combined with its green setting come together to form a 'postcard-perfect' scene, unexpected for this area. St Anne's is built around a cruciform plan with a prominent central crossing tower, with wooden belfry stage and a large central

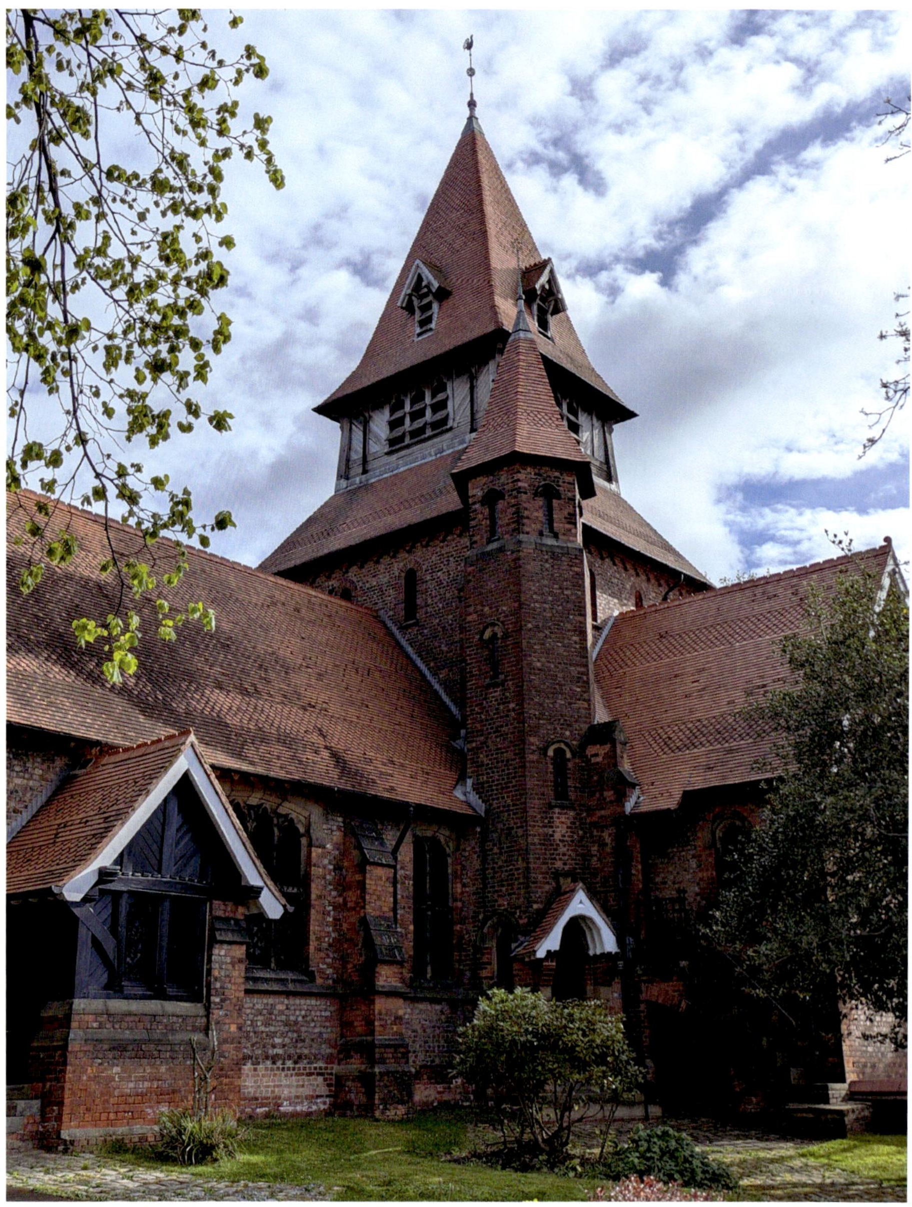

Looking south-east towards the central tower of St Anne's Church, Haughton, Denton.

worship space with transepts. The plan contains vernacular elements such as the ornate brick chimney to the vestry, external stair set to the first-floor level above the undercroft and painted soffits on the gable ends of dormer windows and porches. An octagonal stair turret with a conical roof on the south-east corner of the central tower is an odd addition, but nevertheless completes the charming aesthetic. The east façade of the chancel offers a view of the window

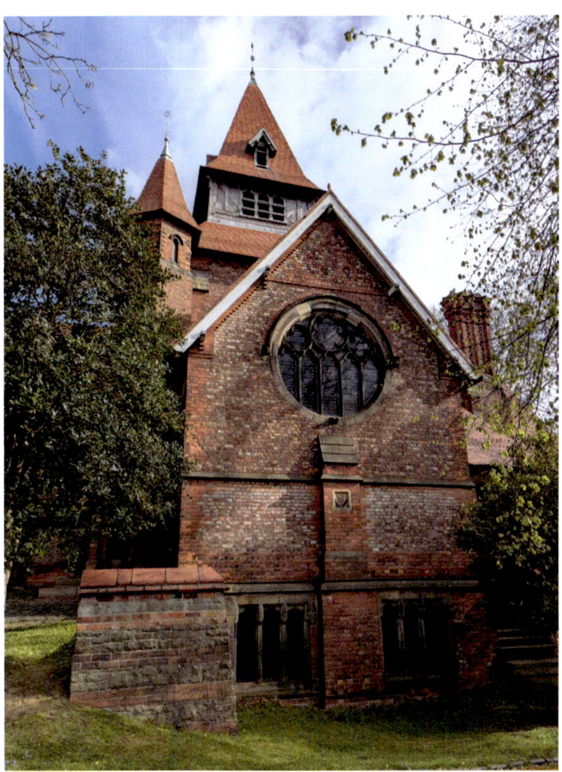

Looking west towards the east
end elevation of St Anne's.

openings giving light to the church's undercroft, and two stages above this is a
rose window with a Gothic tracery.

The whole interior is rich in the artistic qualities of its furnishings and fittings
from stained glass, ironwork, stonework and ceramic details. St Anne's Church
is also notable as one of the architect brothers' most imaginative entirely new
church commissions, showing individuality in its design and craftsmanship.

12. DENTON, ST LAWRENCE

Colloquially known as 'Th' Owd Peg' because it was held together with wooden
pegs, St Lawrence's Church could not feel more lost in its modern setting and
stands as an unusual relic of a bygone time on a small green junction, shoulder to
shoulder with mid-century housing estates, off-licences and sports playing fields.
It is said to be the only surviving timber-framed church in south-east Lancashire.
The former chapel was granted parochial status in its own right in 1854, shortly
before it was substantially reordered inside, being originally a chapel of ease
dating to *c.* 1530 of which a dozen bays of original timber survive in the central
worship space. Above the main entrance, the gable overhangs the west door,
topped with a small bellcote and giving the impression of a church in the rural
pastoral south rather than Greater Manchester. That is also to say that both of
the Anglican churches in Denton (the other being St Anne's, Haughton) are of a

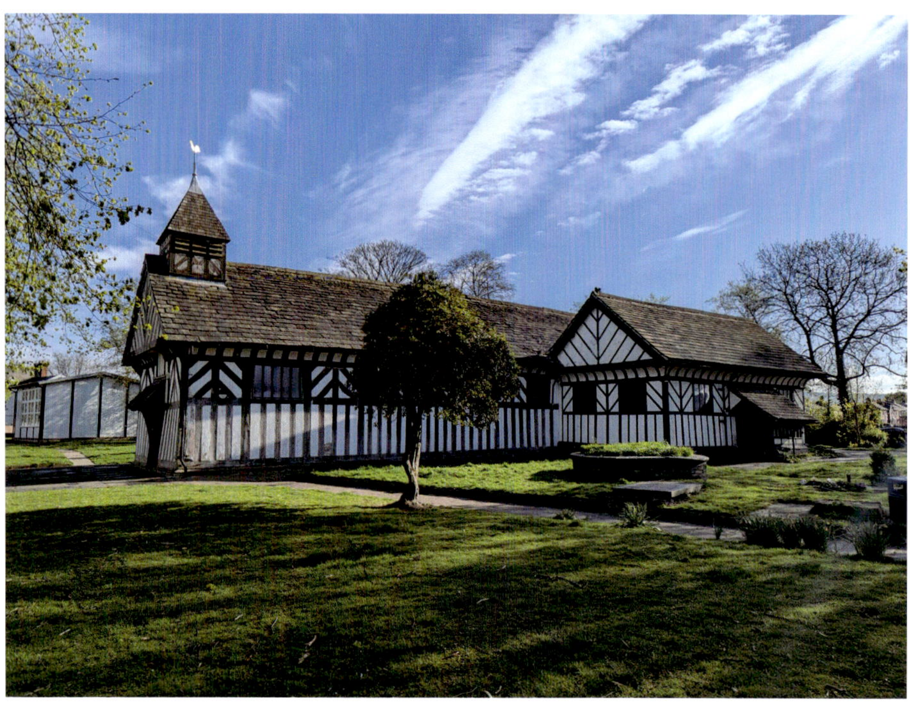

St Lawrence's, Denton.

most unusual character for their present settings. But we must remember until not that long ago, outlying areas of Manchester around its satellite towns and villages were largely fields and farmland.

The architect brothers James Medland Taylor and Henry Taylor, who worked extensively on new and existing church buildings in this parish during the second half of the nineteenth century, made sensitive alterations to this small, charming church, reworking the chancel and transepts in 1872. Further restorations retain the character of this unique timber-framed structure. Part of the nave south wall was repaired from 2002 to 2003, when original timbers were found beneath plasterwork showing that the pattern of painted timbers followed an original scheme. It is not to be confused with the nearby church of St Mary's at Haughton Green, which is not medieval and dates from 1874 to 1876, also by James Medland Taylor and Henry Taylor, which was designed in imitation of St Lawrence's Church.

13. Eccles, St Andrew

St Andrew's Church consists of a wide-aisled, seven-bay nave designed by architect Herbert Edward Tijou. The external character is at first impression one of rudimentary Victorian stoicism, although the bell tower is interesting as it does not form part of the structure of the central worship space. Rather, it appears to be freestanding and detached from the nave, but it is in fact linked by a short link passage. The grand bell tower was added by architect Joseph Stretch Crowther a decade after work on the nave and chancel was under way in 1879. Despite its highly listed status at Grade II*, St Andrew's Church might be overlooked by visitors as a somewhat ordinary Gothic Revival church on the outskirts of a predominantly modern town. The church is, in my opinion, a bit of a hidden gem. One of particular appeal to those with an interest in Victorian stained glass by the eminent glazing firms of the second half of the nineteenth century.

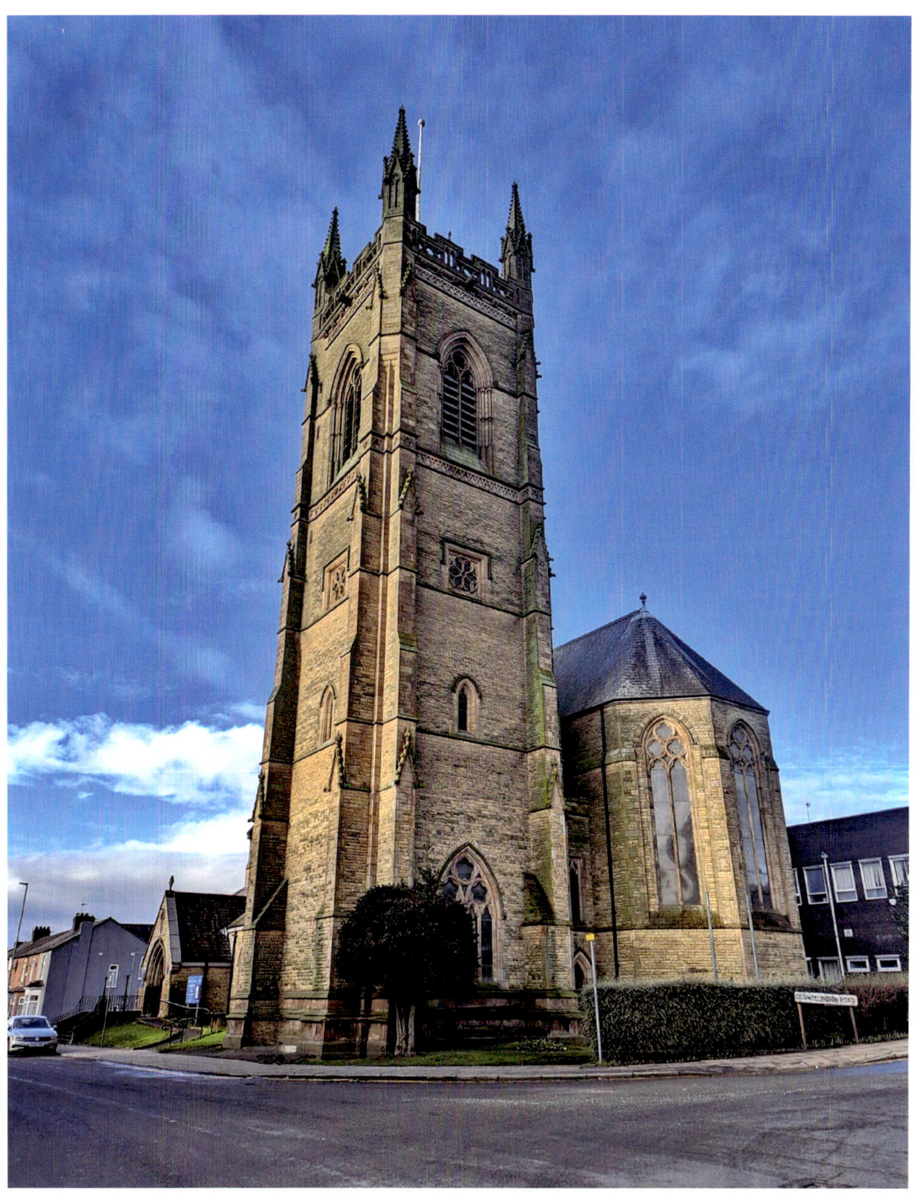

St Andrew's, Eccles.

This large church would have once been heavily pewed prior to the removal of several rows of benches from the west end of the nave. The pews in the aisles were introduced after their removal from Manchester Cathedral in 1893. The pews in the centre of the nave are of lesser artistic interest and historic significance and were introduced in 1918. The overall appearance of the interior setting is sparse until you reach the elaborate chancel, raised by three steps in the ecclesiologist fashion, with richly carved blind arcade panelling surrounding the reredos and parclose screens behind elaborate and good-quality choir stalls. However, the

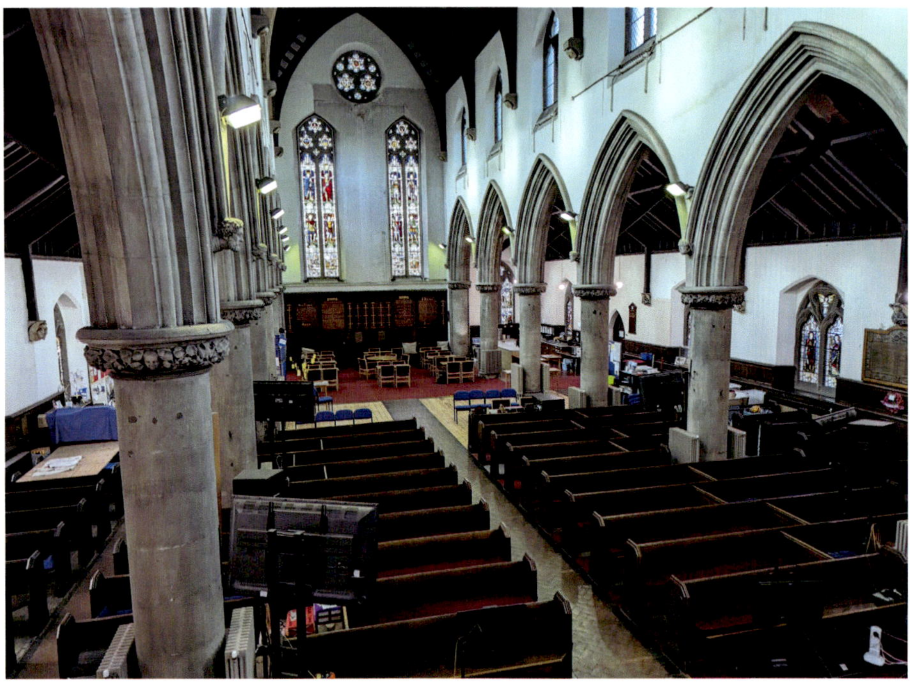

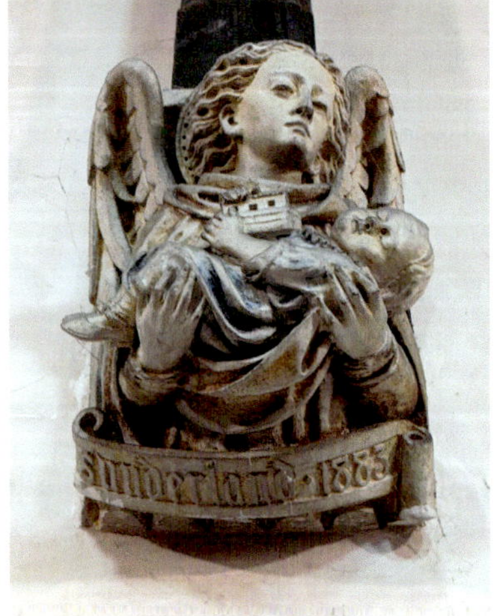

Above: Interior of St Andrew's, looking west from the organ console level.

Left: Victoria Hall memorial, St Andrew's, Eccles.

church has been reordered several times and the absence of windows in the apsed chancel does beg the question of whether this space has lost some portion of its original decorative scheme. It has, and the church has been reordered several times since. Most recently in the 1960s, and it is deeply regrettable that a series of colourful murals depicting figures such as Queen Victoria, soldiers, nurses and biblical scenes by artist Alfred Octavius Hemming were painted over. Four of Hemming's stained-glass windows remain, in addition to windows by other eminent Victorian glazing firms such as Shrigley and Hunt of Lancaster and Charles Eamer Kempe of London. These windows add a splash of colour to an otherwise whitewashed interior, absent of embellishment. It is in one window specifically that a particular point of interest can be seen. In the north aisle is a war memorial window in commemoration of Arthur Handley Clayton, of this parish, who was killed in France at the Battle of Loos on 25 September 1915, aged twenty-three. This window is special as it also depicts Arthur with what we must assume is a likeness to the man himself, dressed in military uniform, deceased, but resting peacefully. The composition is sombre and a poignant artwork for reflection. It is rich in detail: from the insignia on his military hat and the barrel of his rifle down to the mud on the bottom of his boots.

Also in the north aisle is a particularly harrowing memorial that has long been overlooked but is entirely deserving of attention. Again, it is a memorial to a tragic event and testimony to the people of this parish wishing to pay their respects to innocent lives lost in a disaster which occurred almost 150 miles away. Here can be seen a painted corbel of an angel cradling a small child clutching a model of Noah's Ark. Beneath are the words 'Sunderland. 1883'. This commemorates the Victoria Hall disaster which occurred on 16 June 1883 at the Victoria Hall in Sunderland (Tyne and Wear). In a devastating incident 183 children lost their lives by being crushed in an oversized crowd during an event to distribute free toys, causing widespread public upset and setting in place motions to change the law regarding public safety in large indoor events.

14. Eccles, St Mary

There are two notable parish churches in Eccles, of which St Mary's is the oldest. St Mary's is in fact the oldest-surviving building in the town and was the only Anglican church in its large parish until the second half of the eighteenth century. As such, it houses notable treasures and numerous features of historical interest.

There is evidence of the development of the original medieval structure, with surviving architecture from almost every period of building between the fourteenth and nineteenth centuries. The external masonry is a mix of blotchy pale red and blackened sandstone. The stain of industry and passage of time has left its mark on susceptible stone. The church was almost entirely externally refaced in 1907 when it was noted that the sandstone masonry was deteriorating and in desperate need for replacement. The dappled masonry on the three main elevations of the handsome fifteenth-century west tower is quite memorable and not altogether unattractive.

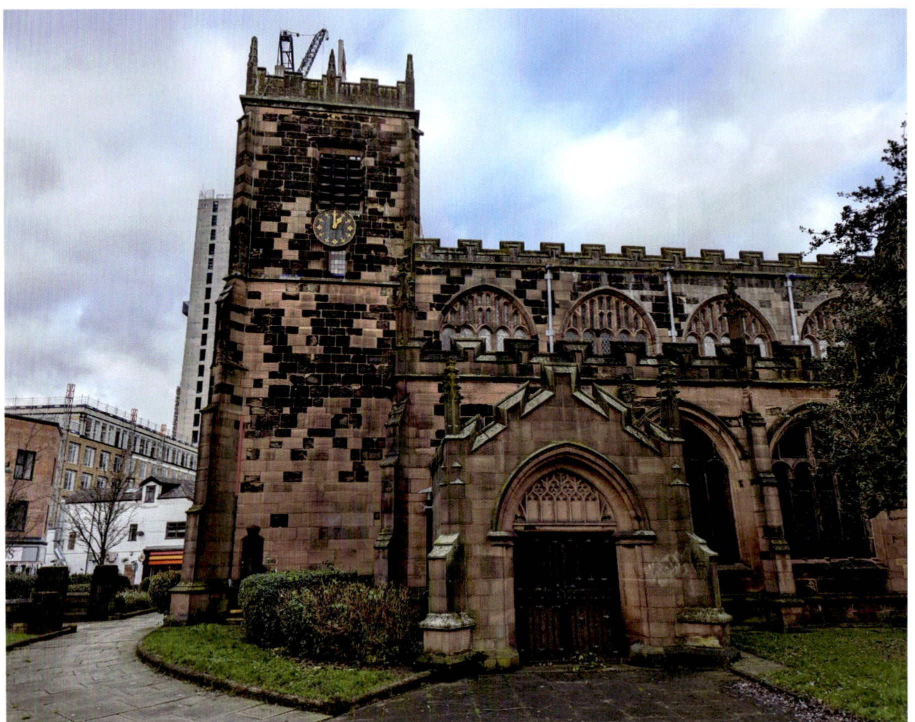

St Mary's, Eccles.

Until relatively recently, access into the church was through the south porch, where visitors and churchgoers would pass through a 600-year-old door consisting of thick oak beams and wrought-iron strap hinges of exceptional medieval craftsmanship. This door can still be seen internally on request. It is the various monuments, objects and furnishings to be found around the building that bring to life the heritage of one of Greater Manchester's oldest towns and the lives of its worshipping communities and worthies alike.

Between 1862 and 1863, much of the eastern part of the building was completely rebuilt. Doubt has been cast on whether this was truly successful as the floor in front of the high altar rail has sunk and the area cordoned off awaiting repair. This does not deter from the setting of the chancel. It is a holistic Victorian scheme and the quality of the carving on the choir stalls and parclose screens to the south and north chapels is hard to fault. The medieval timber nave roof may be late fifteenth century in date, and the nave arcades with the clerestory above added only a little later.

A terrific Elizabethan tomb with three stone effigies is one of the finest of its kind in Greater Manchester. The Brereton tomb was moved into St Katherine's Chapel with the creation of the Bridgewater Centre community room in 1996, where it originally stood in the former south chapel in front of the east window. The inscription running around the stone tabletop records the deaths of Sir Richard Brereton of Tatton and Worsley (d. 1598), his wife Dorothy (d. 1639) and their

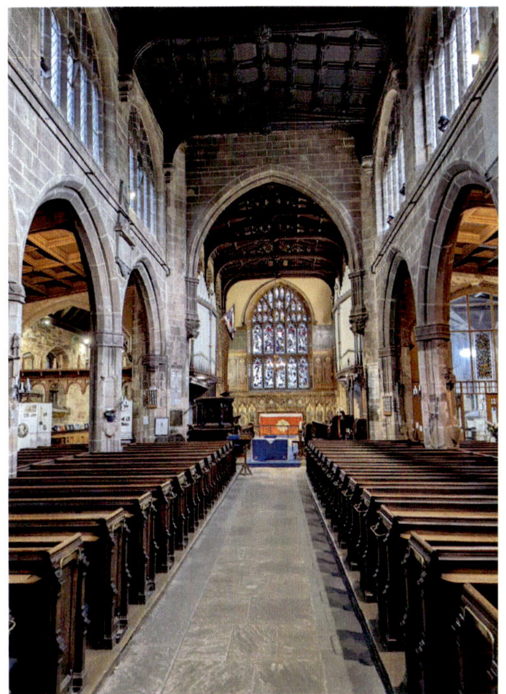
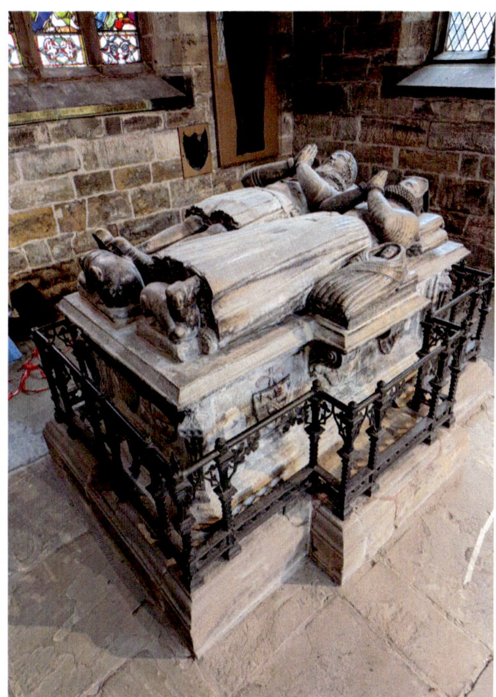

Above left: Interior of St Mary's, looking east.

Above right: The Brereton tomb, St Mary's, Eccles.

stillborn son Richard (d. 1575). Dorothy was the daughter of Sir Richard Egerton of Ridley; she arranged for this fine tomb to be erected in 1600. Before leaving the chapel, the reader should take notice of three coffin lids with their original name plates, each dating from the eighteenth and early nineteenth centuries. It is an unusual opportunity to see coffin lids, which are normally locked away or concealed underground in burial vaults.

St Mary's is plentiful with coloured glass in its aisle windows. Two windows in particular are of individual interest, although they are separated by 500 years in date. The first is the so-called 'Long Donkey Window' in the west wall of the south aisle. This sixteenth-century stained-glass window depicts Christ's entry into Jerusalem. However, the poor donkey's body is spread across three lights in a wide, five-light window and was obviously never meant to fill a window of this scale or design. Despite its comical appearance the overall composition is clearly sophisticated, with organic and architectural features in the background, enriching the scene and setting of the church, not least for its bold colours. It was removed from a convent in Rouen (France) and originally installed in another church in Manchester until demolition in 1929 after which it was moved to Eccles. It is comparable to another sixteenth-century stained-glass window in Lichfield Cathedral (Staffordshire) also depicting Christ's entry into Jerusalem, removed from the Cistercian convent at Herkenrode, Flanders (Belgium). The second

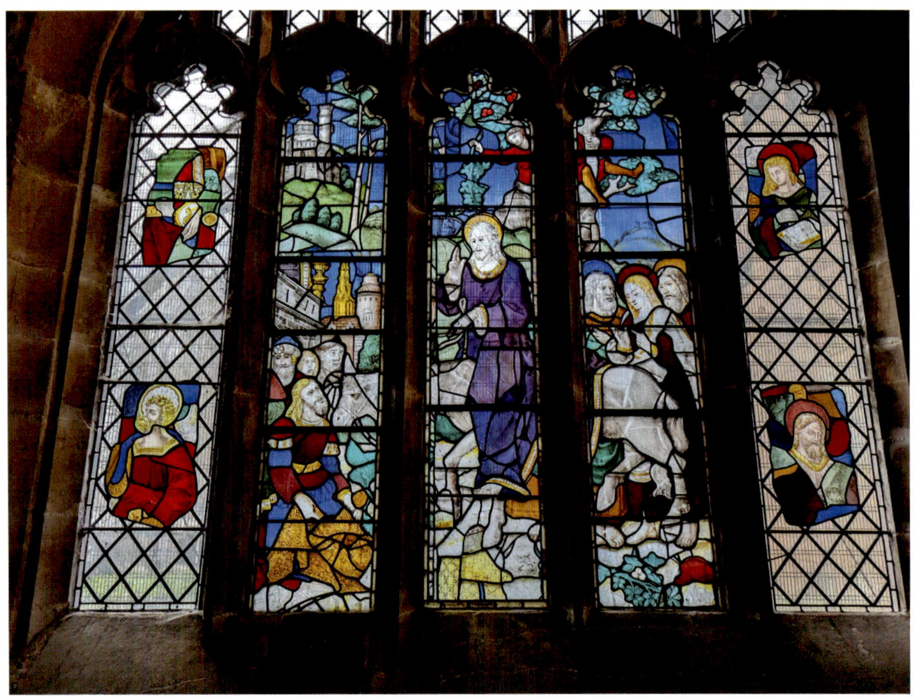

Christ's entry into Jerusalem window, St Mary's, Eccles.

window in St Mary's Church worth seeking out is a short walk across to the west wall of the north aisle for the memorial window installed in memory of William Worrel Mayo, founder of the Mayo Clinic in America, installed in 1929 and designed by glazier Francis Spear.

15. EDGELEY ST MATTHEW

A traditional Gothic Revival church by architect Joseph Stretch Crowther serving the terraced streets of Edgeley on the south-west side of Stockport railway station. St Matthew's sits within a neat, green lawnscape occupying a similar size plot to one of the adjacent rows of houses. There are no burials within the churchyard, no memorials nor headstones and an absence of trees (albeit some blossom lining the path to the west entrance) which although regrettable for not beautifying its setting, shows that uninterrupted elevations of the building can be obtained from all sides. The church was built in 1855 with the tower and spire added a decade later, completing the uniform and near enough symmetrical ground plan consisting of a high-pitched aisled nave with two aisles, a chancel, north-east vestry and south porch.

A sense of incredible space within is due to the design and subsequent treatment of the high ceilings. The internal walls of the nave, aisles and chancel are all rendered white, throwing greater definition upon the beams of the two scissor-braced roofs in the nave and chancel. Complementing this is the treatment of

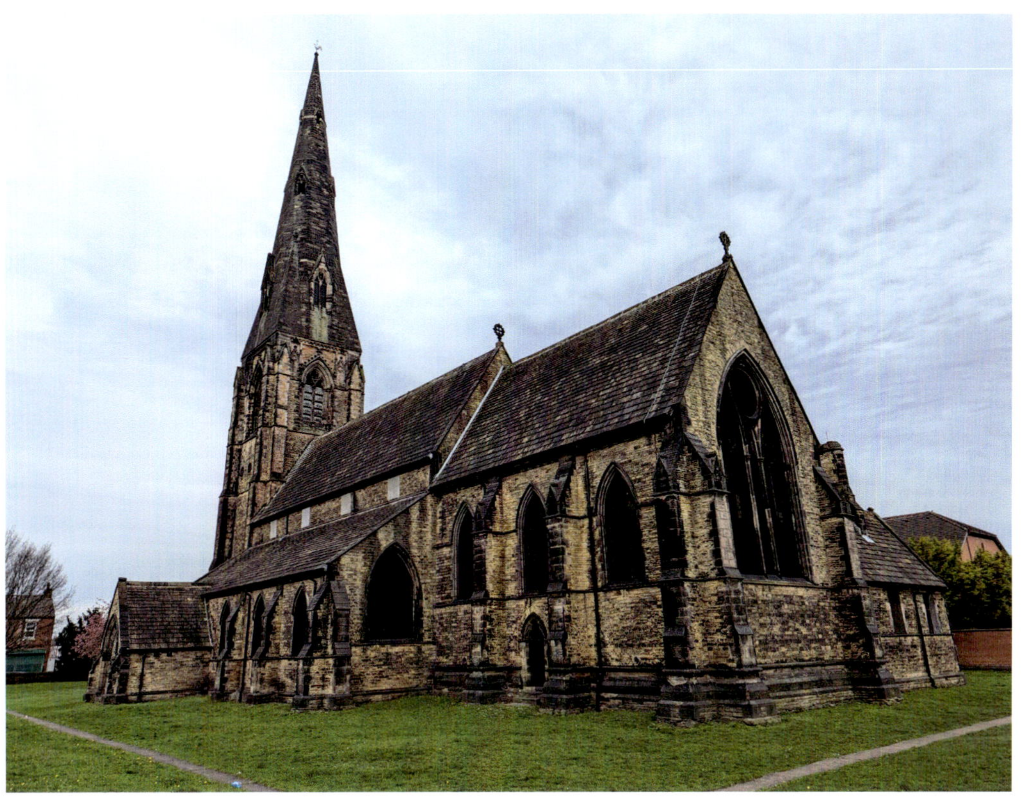

St Matthew's Church, Edgeley.

exposed stone quoins around the internal window reveals. It is simple but effective. The church is quite densely pewed but reasonably accessible. Step-free access to the nave dais allows for a free flow around the building. Much of this is a result of a reordering in the early 1990s, which included the removal of several pews at the west end of the nave and the adaptation of the south porch to accommodate a toilet, none of which greatly spoiled the integrity of the building and the remaining original furnishings. There are some very fine stained-glass windows in the church and a walk around to inspect them each in turn is encouraged. The east window is believed to be the work of Heaton, Butler and Bayne of London. Hardman & Co., and Abbot & Co. of Lancaster glass adorns windows in the nave aisles.

16. Fairfield Moravian Church

Established in 1785, the Fairfield Moravian settlement is a significant example of eighteenth-century Moravian communal life in England. The Moravian Church is a Protestant denomination of Christianity with roots in the Bohemian Reformation of the early fifteenth century. Founded in Droylsden by Revd Benjamin Latrobe, a key figure in the Moravian Church in England, the settlement was designed as a self-contained community centered around the Moravian chapel. The commune

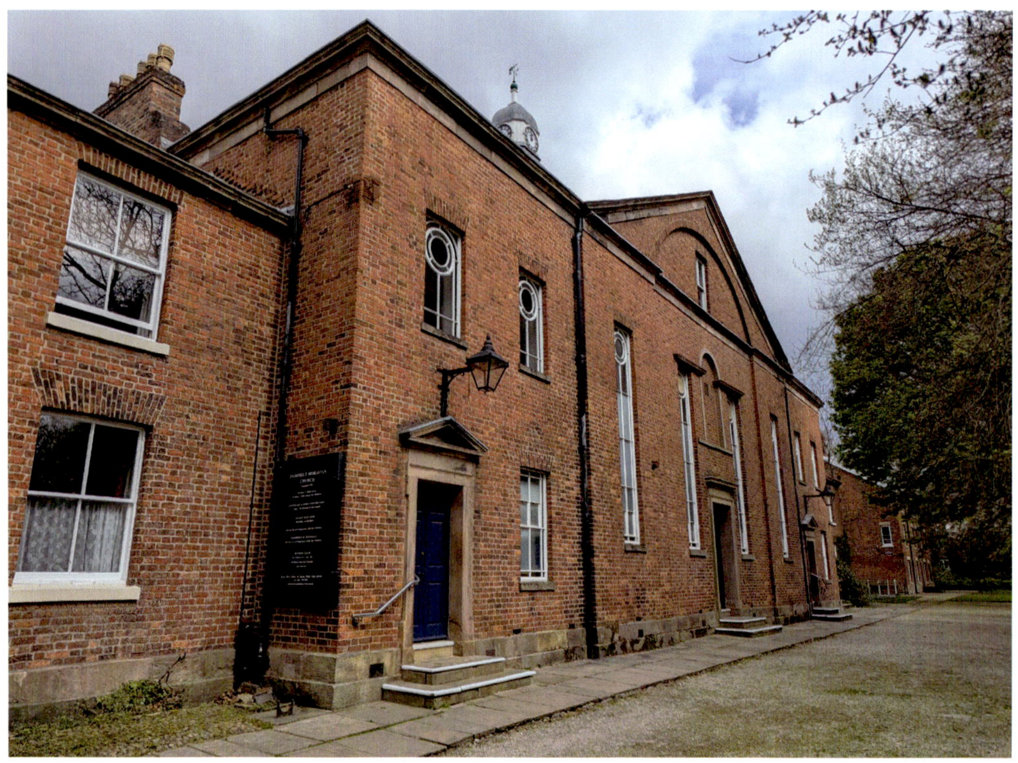

Fairfield Moravian Church.

is reminiscent of the slightly earlier Fulneck Moravian settlement in the village of Pudsey (West Yorkshire).

The settlement was designed by John Lees, a Moravian architect from Oldham. The community was laid out around a large central square, with the chapel on the south side overlooking well-kept private gardens and a burial ground known as 'God's Acre'. Built around the square are houses, originally for brothers and sisters of the community, as well as married couples, reflecting the Moravian practice of communal living in 'choirs'. Choirs were not to do with singing in this context, but was the name given to a system of social order within the community in which members of each group or 'choir' were all of a similar sex, age and marital status. These groups were small spiritual families, who each lived and worshiped together. An example of different choirs would be those for children, married men, married women and even a widows choir, amongst others, depending on the size of the settlement.

The Fairfield Chapel, house and manse were all built in 1785, and the chapel was consecrated in July the same year with a grand public opening which attracted around 1,500 attendees. Approached from Brethren Court or Sisters Street to the north and south, respectively, the first impression is of a broad building with three south-facing entrances and thin windows beneath a giant, brick-faced pediment. It is of header-bonded brick and stone dressings to the cornice, door surrounds and ground plinth.

The small clock turret atop the chapel features a relatively rare clock mechanism by William Groves of Leeds. Groves was a bellringer at Leeds Parish Church (West Yorkshire) and he had a shop on Kirkgate only a short distance from that church. Just two other clocks by him are widely known; one survives at Christ Church Mount Pellon near Halifax (West Yorkshire) and a record of a lost clock at St Peter's Church in Earlsheaton (West Yorkshire), now demolished. In its setting amongst houses, a college and other buildings of the eighteenth century is an experience of religious communal living unique in Greater Manchester.

The chapel in no way seeks to stand out from other buildings in the settlement. Inside are a series of timber glazed screens, pews and panelling. Virtually all of the church's internal features date from a reordering of 1908.

17. FALINGE, ST EDMUND

Rochdale's so-called 'Temple to Freemasonry', St Edmund's Church, stands in a diamond-shaped churchyard at the convergence of four roads in the suburb of Falinge not far from Rochdale town centre. St Edmund's is noteworthy for its uncompromising storytelling through stone and physical form. Here you will find the visual and moral code of Freemasonry set out in sculpture and architecture.

Externally, it is both a beautiful and brazen example of Victorian Gothic Revival architecture, but there is something unequivocally severe about this building. Walking a full lap of the curtilage, the reader will notice it has the footprint of a Latin cross. It is also apparent that it appears impenetrable, like a castle, in an elevated position and set upon a continuous battered plinth. The buttresses and the turret are also built on battered plinths. In this sense it feels fortified. Small square headed windows contain beautiful traceries formed of stars. Step inside the building and there is a clear Arts and Crafts touch upon the larger part of the furnishings and fittings that seems never ending. St Edmund's Church is certainly unique in English ecclesiastical architecture.

In 2007, the church closed for worship and was vested into the care of the Churches Conservation Trust. St Edmund's is occasionally a venue for concerts and other events, with regular open days for visitors and a warm welcome guaranteed every time. At some point the five-pointed star weathervane which once sat upon the central tower was taken down and is now displayed within the church. Whether it will be reinstated is unknown.

St Edmund's was founded at a cost of £20,000 paid for by wealthy banker, industrialist and distinguished Freemason, Albert Hudson Royds. It was built between 1870 and 1873 to a design ultimately conceived in collaboration with the architect Medland Taylor, whose original architectural drawings had no masonic symbolism or decoration, with input from Royds and the church's first incumbent, Revd E. W. Gilbert, who was an artist in his own right and contributed a design for an elaborate reredos which was installed and remains in-situ to this day.

There are masonic forms and symbols stamped on every surface of the furnishings and fittings, and illustrated in a full scheme of stained glass, to put one in the mind of Solomon's Temple in Jerusalem. Look closely and there are thought to be more symbols of Freemasonry than Christianity. The longer one

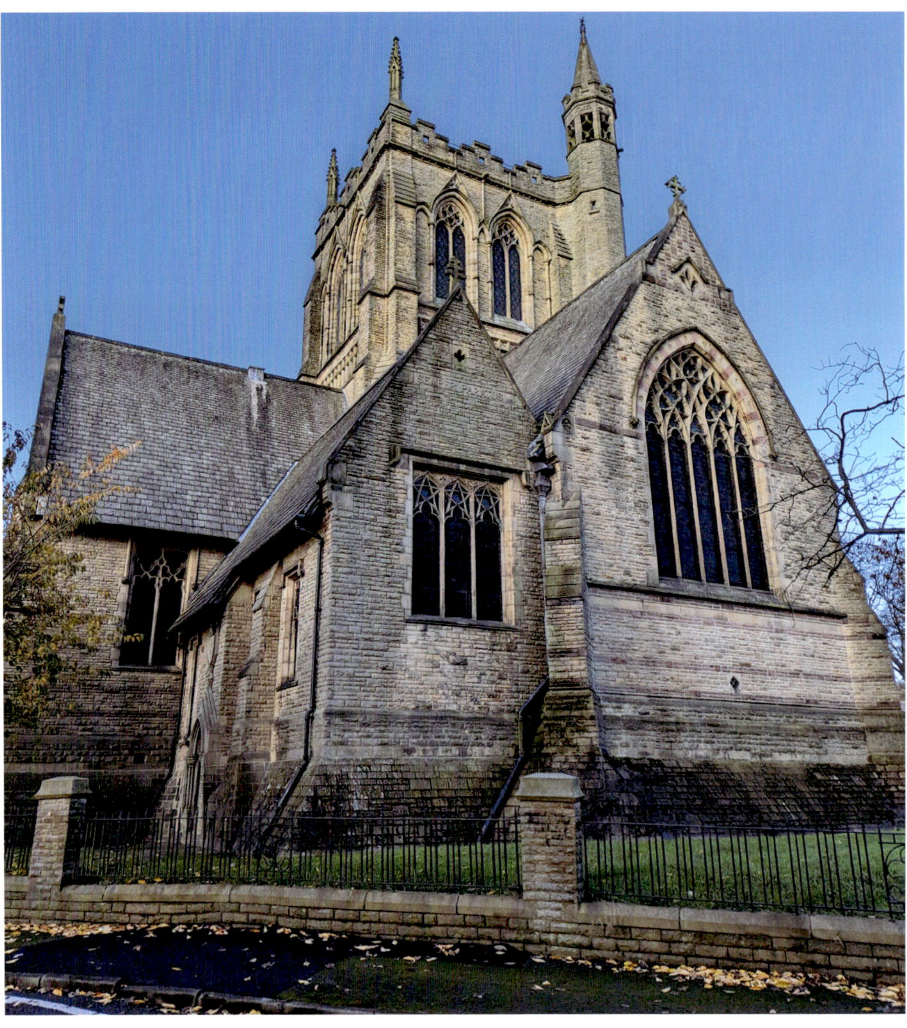

St Edmund's Church, Falinge.

spends studying the building in detail, the easier it is to believe that this may be true. Nowhere is this more plain to see than the wonderful lectern.

The symbolic lectern from which a mason would read the Scriptures is formed of perfectly cut stone blocks. Everything else about it is brass, including brass pillars representing Wisdom, Strength and Beauty in the form of Ionic, Doric and Corinthian columns. Wisdom to contrive, strength to support and beauty to adorn. These pillars support a plate upon which are intricately worked symbols such as the pomegranate and a snake with its tail in its mouth. These ancient symbols are drawn directly from antiquity. The pomegranate was frequently used by masons and can be found on such ornaments adorning the tops or heads of columns. The serpent can appear depicted in several different ways, but when it has its tail in its mouth, it is an emblem of eternity. The slanted book rest is clearly and cleverly worked in the

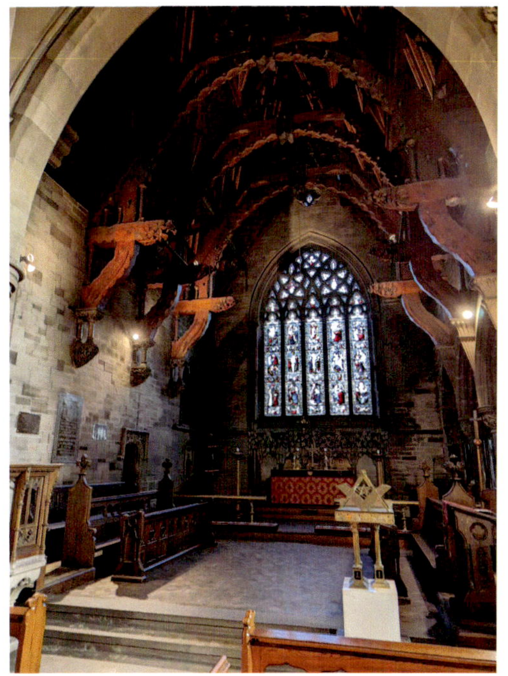

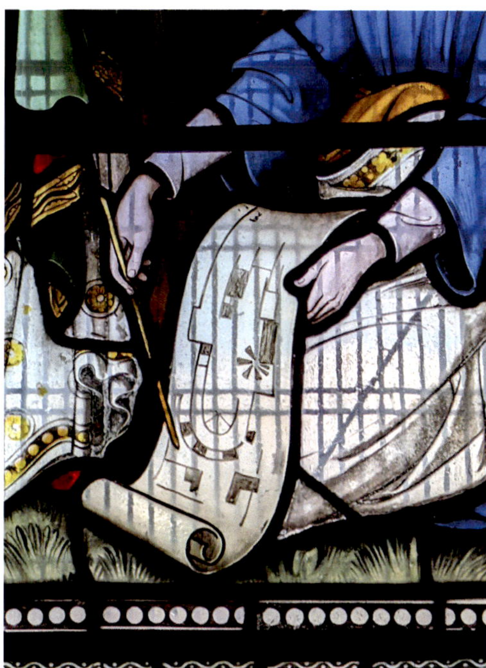

Above left: Interior of St Edmund's, looking east.

Above right: Detail of a stained-glass window showing the plans for building Solomon's Temple, St Edmund's.

Right: Masonic lectern, St Edmund's.

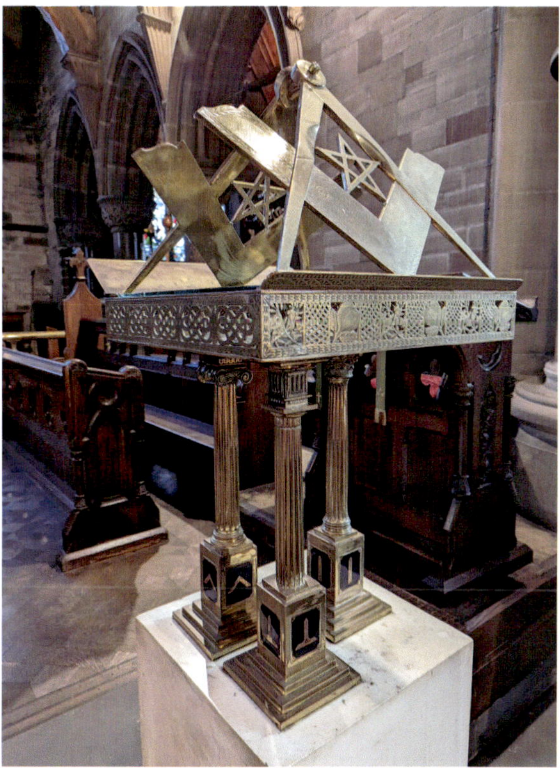

shape of a mason's square and compass, within which is contained a blazing star. There is another star within the lower plate itself between two panes of glass.

All things considered, this is one church in Greater Manchester that should not be missed.

18. GORTON MONASTERY

Standing high above surrounding residential estates, Gorton Monastery is a prominent landmark unlike any other in the local area and for those arriving or departing from Manchester Piccadilly railway station. Arguably one of the most important Roman Catholic churches in the north of England, it has long been celebrated for both its religious and architectural significance but could have been lost entirely following an act of extreme vandalism nearly sealed its fate for good a couple of decades ago. By that point the building had already been standing derelict for nearly a decade and so an urgent appeal was made to determine its future once and for all. The story of the Gorton Monastery's revival after closure as a place of worship in 1989 is unparalleled in Greater Manchester and it is becoming more widely known as a heritage centre and events venue after it was drastically transformed and reopened to the public from 2007.

Originally a Franciscan friary dedicated to St Francis, this iconic building was built for the Order of St Francis to designs by Edward Welby Pugin in a late thirteenth-century Gothic medieval style, between 1864 and 1872. The church stood at the very centre of a working-class, low-income community for almost 130 years. A beautiful building of red brick with generous stone dressings and a street facing elevation with three flying buttresses elegantly rooted into the former entrance porch beneath. The unforgettable spire crowning the spectacular façade was built in 1911 measuring roughly 80 feet in height. Once included on Historic England's Heritage at Risk Register and the World Monuments Fund 100 most endangered sites, the building has been extensively restored and adapted with a new state-of-the-art visitor entrance and now operates with a secular, community use as a conference and events space. The cloister attached to the east side of the church contains a neat courtyard garden and well-maintained green space with many benches where visitors can stop and take a minute in which can also be observed the elevation of the length of the church building itself. The combined total number of clerestory and aisle windows is quite a sight, and it is from here the reader may truly appreciate the depth of this grand building as well as its strong vertical qualities which are more evident from the street.

Before the building reopened in 2011, work to preserve the former worship space focused on retaining as much of the original building fabric and stabilising the existing structure as much as was possible. This included conserving and repairing the stained glass in the three windows of the apsidal chancel and restoring the wide roofs. Unfortunately, many furnishings and fittings were lost and the church itself has no fixed pews or other kind of seating, utilising stackable chairs and tables for its current events package. The elaborate stone reredos designed by the architect's half-brother, Peter Paul Pugin, was victim to vandalism when the building was previously left in a derelict state, and the decision to not restore the

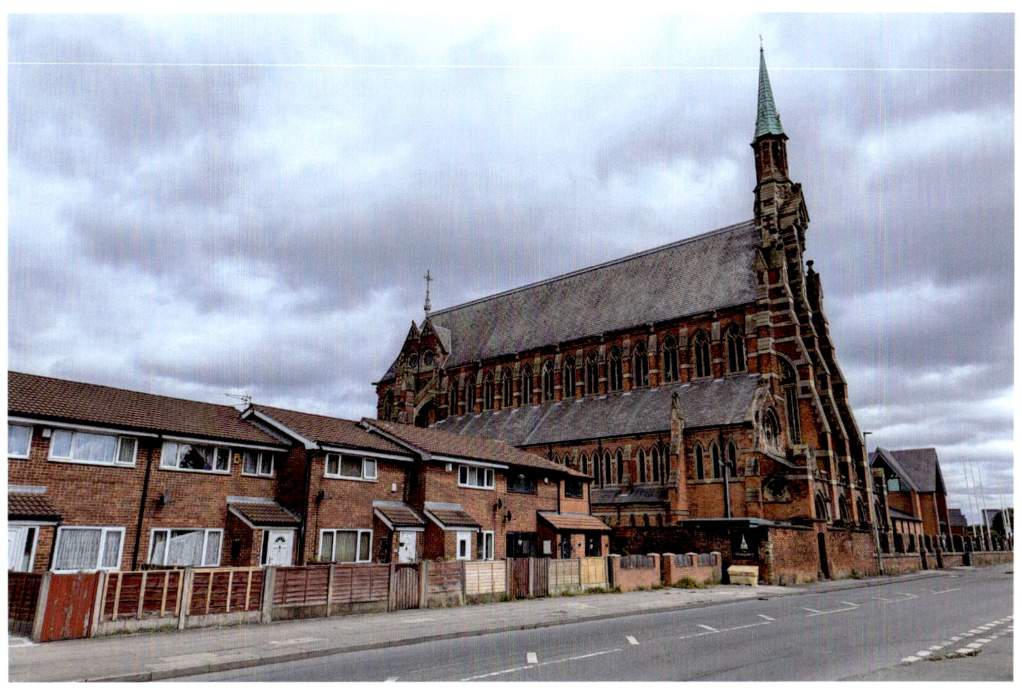

Above and below left: Gorton Monastery.

Below right: Interior of Gorton Monastery, looking east.

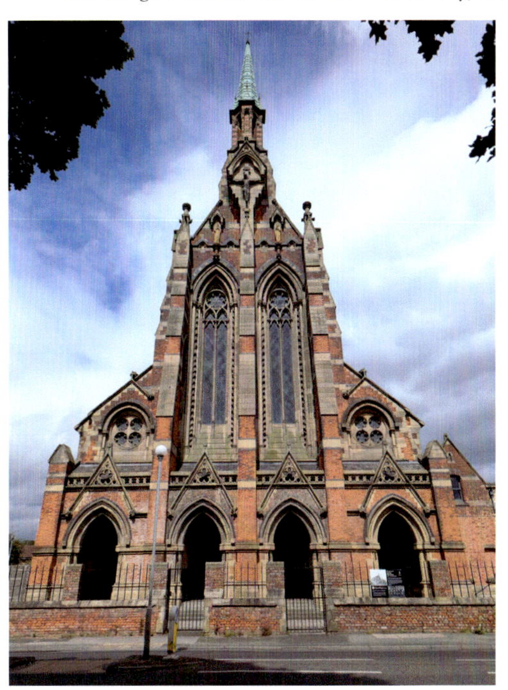

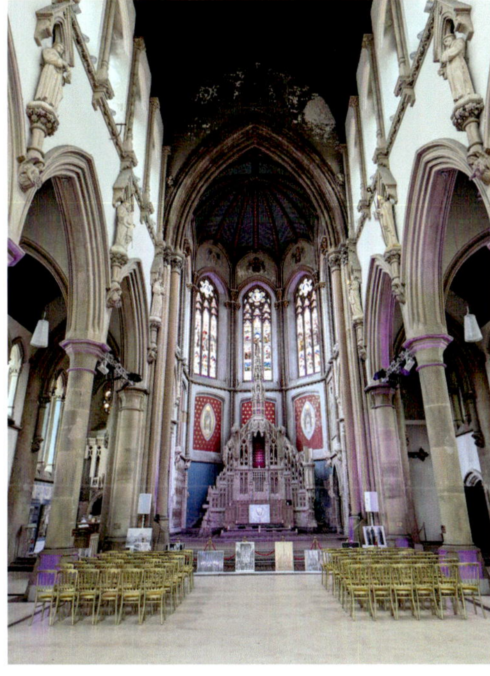

pieces of it which were lost was a bold and positive one. It is no longer an elaborate and complete centrepiece, but its presence is enough to allude to the splendour of its architectural setting at the east end of the church, surrounded at one time by intricate woodwork, statutory and stunning vaulted ceilings. The latter survives today and contained beneath, around the reredos in the sanctuary, is evidence of the original decorative and quite striking colour scheme.

19. MANCHESTER, HIGH BLACKLEY, ST CLARE

St Clare's Church is in my opinion one of the most striking examples of post-war Roman Catholic church design in Greater Manchester, and a building not easily forgotten. Two foundation stones set into the red-brick west façade denote a service of blessing led by the Bishop of Salford which took place on Sunday 11 August 1957 in commemoration of the 50th anniversary of the return of the Grey Friars to England. The dedication to St Clare is appropriate as she was one

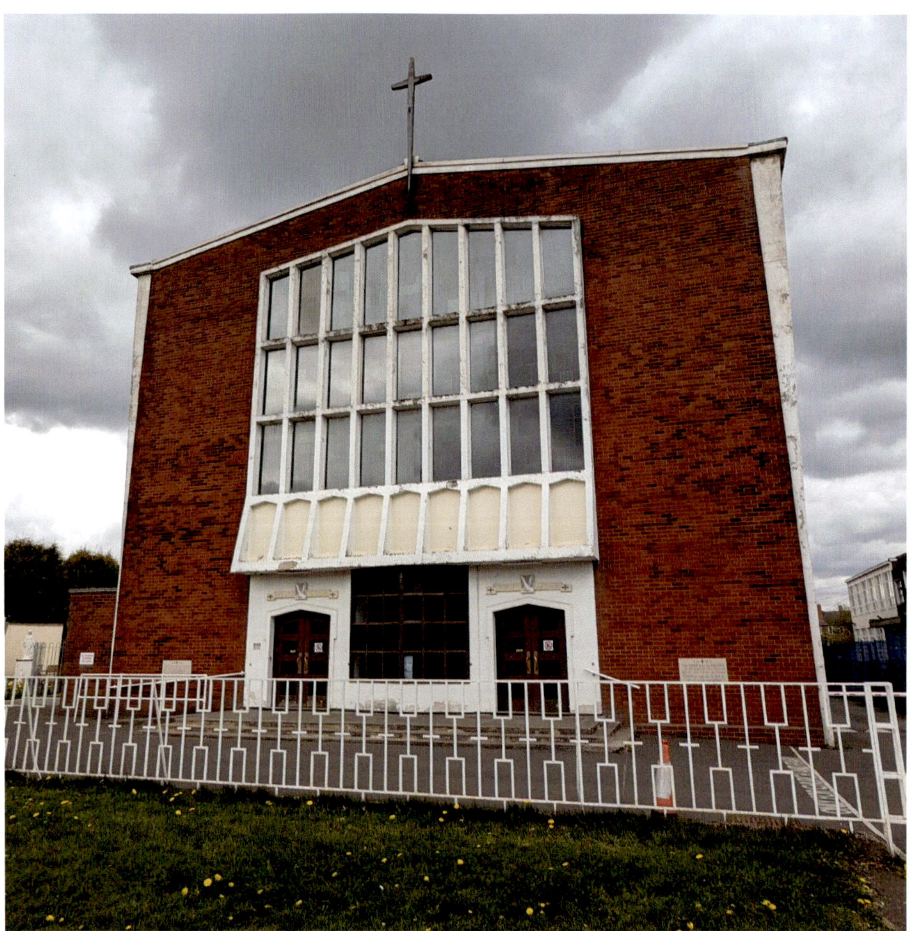

St Clare's, High Blackley, Manchester.

of the first followers of Francis of Assisi, who founded the religious order of the Franciscans.

The basilica-style church facing Victoria Avenue today is the second church on this site, replacing a temporary brick church built in 1929 and after the residential housing estates around Blackley expanded in the first couple of decades of the twentieth century. The interior has not been altered greatly in approaching seventy years, but like many modernist churches of this time, it is beginning to show its age.

The church was designed by A. G. Bullen of Weightman & Bullen. St Clare's was fitted out with a number of furnishings, but when entering the church today it is the grand east end mosaic by artist and teacher Georg Mayer-Marton which demands attention. A pioneer of the art of Byzantine-inspired mosaics, Mayer-Marton was a Jewish refugee who taught at the Liverpool College of Art from 1952. Mayer-Morton's work has been more widely recognised in recent years. The Roman Catholic church of the Holy Rosary in Fitton Hill, a large post-war housing estate south of Oldham which was opened only a couple of years before St Clare's in High Blackley, was recently listed Grade II by Historic England in 2022 and incorporates a significant mural by Mayer-Marton. The mural at Fritton Hill was described 'as a striking aesthetic combination of neo-baroque mosaic and modernist Cubist-influenced fresco'. It is regrettable that the church

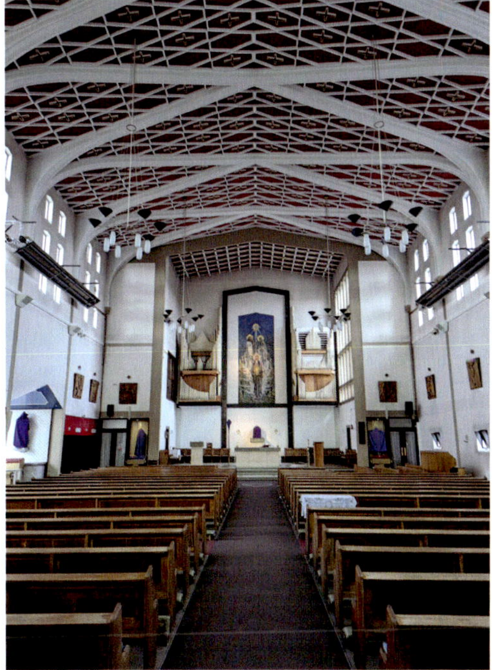

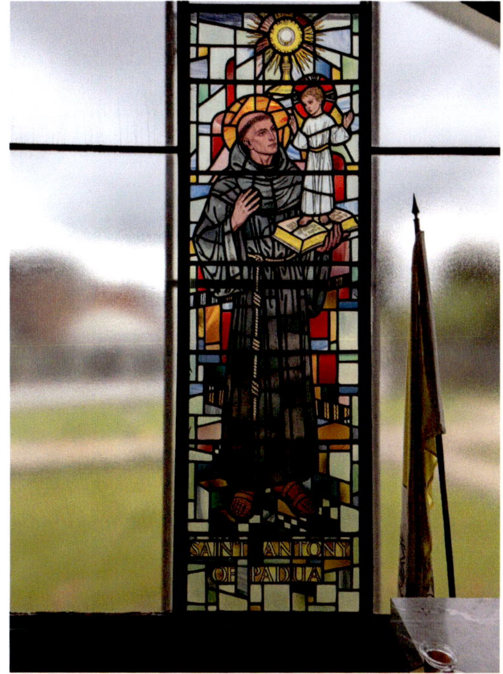

Above left: Interior of St Clare's, looking east.

Above right: St Antony of Padua window by Joseph Edward Nüttgens at St Clare's, High Blackley.

on Fitton Hill, Oldham, is not currently open for inspection. However, the mosaic over the high altar here in St Clare's Church depicting St Clare of Assisi raising the Blessed Sacrament is a remarkable example of Mayer-Marton's mastery of his craft and a triumph of modernist church embellishment. There is a stone font at the front of the south side of the central worship space with brightly coloured mosaic panels of fairly routine symbolism, but it is unclear whether this is also the work of Mayer-Marton.

The setting of St Clare's Church on Victoria Avenue gives little away to the depth of its overall footprint. It is a building of grand proportions. If one makes use of the church car park behind the church set back from the road, it is possible to appreciate its scale more openly, but otherwise one steps from a small entrance into a wide aisleless nave, with three side chapels on the north side and a square-ended sanctuary. The elaborate ribbed ceiling is unforgettable. Concrete divisions painted white on red is an idea drawn from Gothic church design, which in this post-war context is not dissimilar in character and design from the nave ceiling at the Anglican church in Woodhall (Pudsey), West Yorkshire, built in 1959 by Bradford architects Barker and Jordan and dedicated to St James the Great.

Stained glass in St Clare's is by Joseph Edward Nüttgens. Three windows in the nave aisle chapels depict the Blessed Agnellus of Pisa (an Italian Franciscan friar), St Anthony of Padua and St Joseph of Cupertino. Around the walls of the church are large Stations of the Cross by David John. Some fittings have been removed as a result of an interior reordering after the Second Vatican Council, but the overall impression of this pleasant modernist church is no less remarkable for it.

20. Manchester, St Mary (Mulberry Street)

Manchester's 'Hidden Gem' is so called for two reasons. On the one hand it is literally hidden. That such a large basilican-form church of the Rhenish Romanesque style, which would otherwise draw attention to itself in a more open urban setting, stands within a densely built-up position surrounded by modern office and retail buildings, unbeknownst to the majority of pedestrians walking past the nearby town hall and square, is remarkable. Secondly, it is so called for its interior ornamentation. Although the church was built and completed in 1848, the term 'Hidden Gem' was used to describe the subsequent embellishment of the church interior several decades later, and the addition of notably high-quality furnishings.

Standing back from Mulberry Street, the main elevation of this red-brick church is remarkably noble, and the high-reaching helm tower an eye-catching, distinctive feature. This was the second church; the need for a replacement came with the partial collapse of its predecessor in 1833. The church we see today was designed by architects Weightman & Hadfield and its architectural significance has been partially attributed to its influential design, with several architectural historians and critics asking whether it influenced the Byzantine design of Westminster Cathedral in London under the instruction of Bishop Vaughan, who knew this church so well when he was Bishop of Salford.

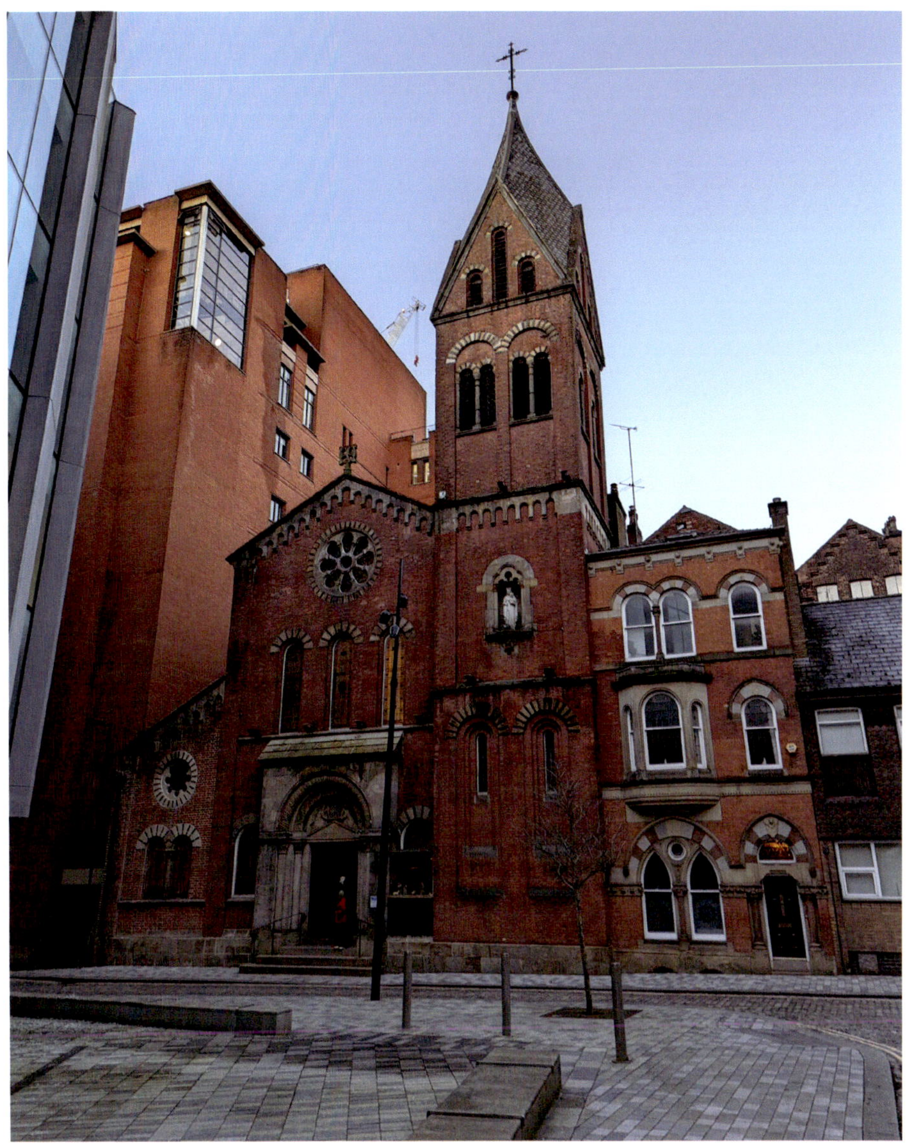

St Mary's, Mulberry Street, Manchester.

One enters the building through a Romanesque stone portal facing out onto Mulberry Street, formed of two decorated arched orders with a central tympanum depicting two angels supporting a central roundel containing the Agnes Dei. The basilican interior has hand painted nave arcade columns which imitate a more costly building material. It is well known that this church was built on a budget with a bare clerestory level and an exposed timber roof with a small lantern oculus. It imbues a sense of calm and contemplation. However, against this rather plain architectural setting are a series of ornate altarpieces and faultless sculptures.

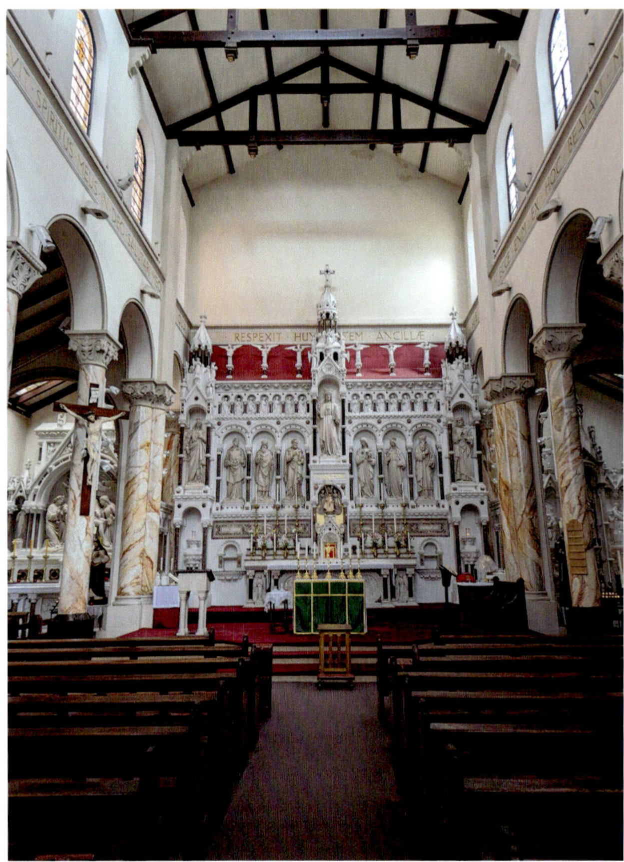

Interior of St Mary's,
looking east.

The length of the sanctuary is almost entirely filled with a great stone and marble reredos adorned with statuary of the Sacred Heart with saints and angels occupying many niches of a vast architectural structure complete with canopied, open turrets. Investment in the 1870s introduced a highly decorative scheme of stone fittings, comprising altars and reredoes by the carver Mr Lane of Preston. The term 'Hidden Gem' was first attributed to Bishop Vaughan, who acquired for this church a medieval font from a church in Germany. Although the church has undergone a reordering and restoration in the years since it was embellished some 150 years ago, it is undoubtedly still deserving of its endearing nickname.

21. MANCHESTER CATHEDRAL

Manchester Cathedral is located north of the modern town centre atop a broad, flat-faced outcrop ('bluff') of sandstone overlooking the confluence of the rivers Irk and Irwell, the former being covered over in the second half of the nineteenth century to make way for a street called Walkers Croft. It is suspected that this is the site of an early church referenced in the Domesday Book, a theory supported by the discovery in February 1871 of a stone panel carved with the relief of an angel, known as the 'Angel Stone'. Recent research has dated the stone to the eleventh or twelfth century, not the seventh century as initially suggested. The presence of what has been described as a runic inscription in one corner of the stone remains unclear, but it is not thought to be runic; in fact it is Latin, and reads: 'Into thy hands, O Lord, I commend my spirit'. The stone is visible behind a glass screen located on the north side of the nave, mounted on one side of a nave arcade pillar.

The site of the church is close to the medieval market area, which by the thirteenth century had a weekly market and an annual fair. This was also the ecclesiastical centre of the old town. It was a nucleus focused around the church, which in 1421, under the appeal of Thomas de la Warre, rector and the lord of the manor, was permitted by royal licence to establish a college of clergy and transform the existing church to a collegiate foundation. The fifteenth-century church was dedicated to three saints – St Mary, St George and St Deny – and was rebuilt at that time befitting its new collegiate status. In the time that has since passed the entire building has altered to such an extent that it is often noted how challenging it can be for the less perceiving eye to distinguish what is genuinely medieval from later work carried out in phases of renovation. This is especially true concerning the exterior fabric of which no medieval stonework survives.

The complete story of the church's renovation and restoration is complicated, but fortunately it is very well documented. In summary, the church was substantially restored following its elevation to cathedral status in the mid-nineteenth century. On 19 April 1847, the Anglican Diocese of Manchester was formed and the former collegiate church of Manchester, with its colourful history, was felt to be the obvious choice for reconstitution as the cathedral church of the new diocese. It was now time for some longstanding and deeply concerning maintenance issues to be addressed, although a general piecemeal approach to undertake isolated repairs is noted to have been underway from *c.* 1815.

It is to the engineering and architectural skill of architect Joseph Stretch Crowther that a scheme of widespread renovations was implemented, resulting in the appearance of the building we see today. Crowther's reconstruction of the nave was perhaps his greatest challenge and his most recognised achievement, replacing entirely the north and south nave arcades and restoring the nave clerestory. The ceiling purportedly reuses original wooden ceiling bosses and angels with relatively little alteration. In 1864, the deconstruction and complete rebuilding of the west tower was underway. It is regrettable that the dilapidated tower fabric, by far the oldest surviving part of the medieval church complete with a fourteenth-century west door, was lost.

Almost sixty years ago Manchester Cathedral was noted by one commentator as 'often overlooked and thought to only be of interest to the fanatic of Victoriana'. This is simply not the case, and one must look east towards the choir to the remarkable collection of furnishings and fittings, comprising the stalls, canopies and screens – plus, of course, the great choir ceiling.

You would be forgiven for not at first observing that much of the east end of the cathedral was greatly rebuilt following significant damage as a result of bombs being dropped on the city during a German air raid in December 1940. Apart from Coventry, no other English cathedral suffered so greatly during a

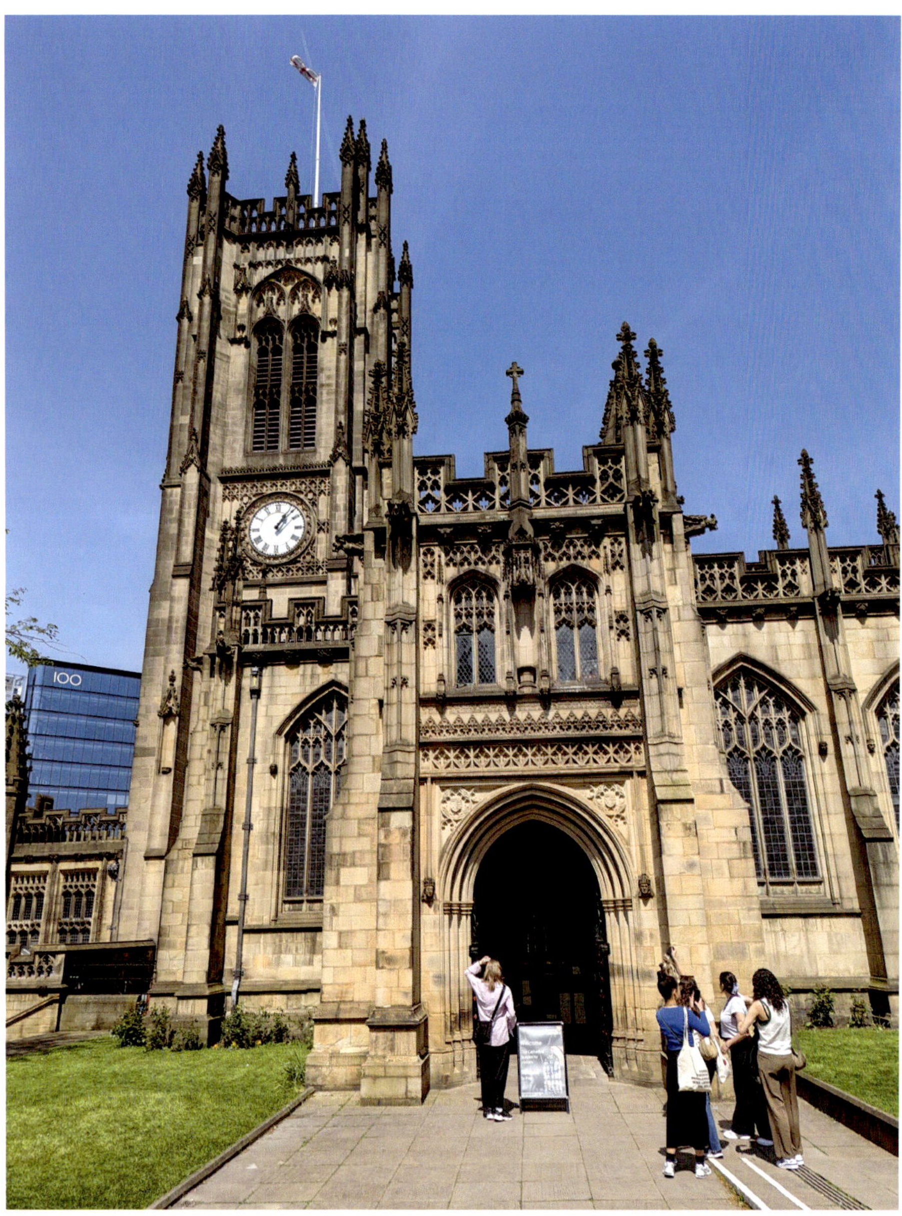

Manchester Cathedral.

Second World War air raid than Manchester. The choir was screened off from the nave and converted into a workshop base for the rebuilding of the now lost Lady and Ely chapels and the restoration of the choir ceiling and choir aisles. The choir ceiling consists of 192 traceried panels, of which 187 required replacement in oak. The restoration is so convincingly in-keeping with the original, owing to the meticulous surveys of the fabric undertaken in previous years by skilled draftsmen, including none other than Joseph Crowther whose book *The Cathedral Church of Manchester* was published in 1893. The detail of the ceiling is illuminated by the large clerestory windows, separated by braces pierced with heraldic devices and cusped internally, supported beneath by angels also carrying heraldic devices. The north and south choir elevations are nothing short of staggering.

The wooden furnishings and fittings at ground level are all worthy of careful study and should not be rushed on inspection. There are a full set of late fifteenth- or early sixteenth-century misericords in the restored choir stalls, which

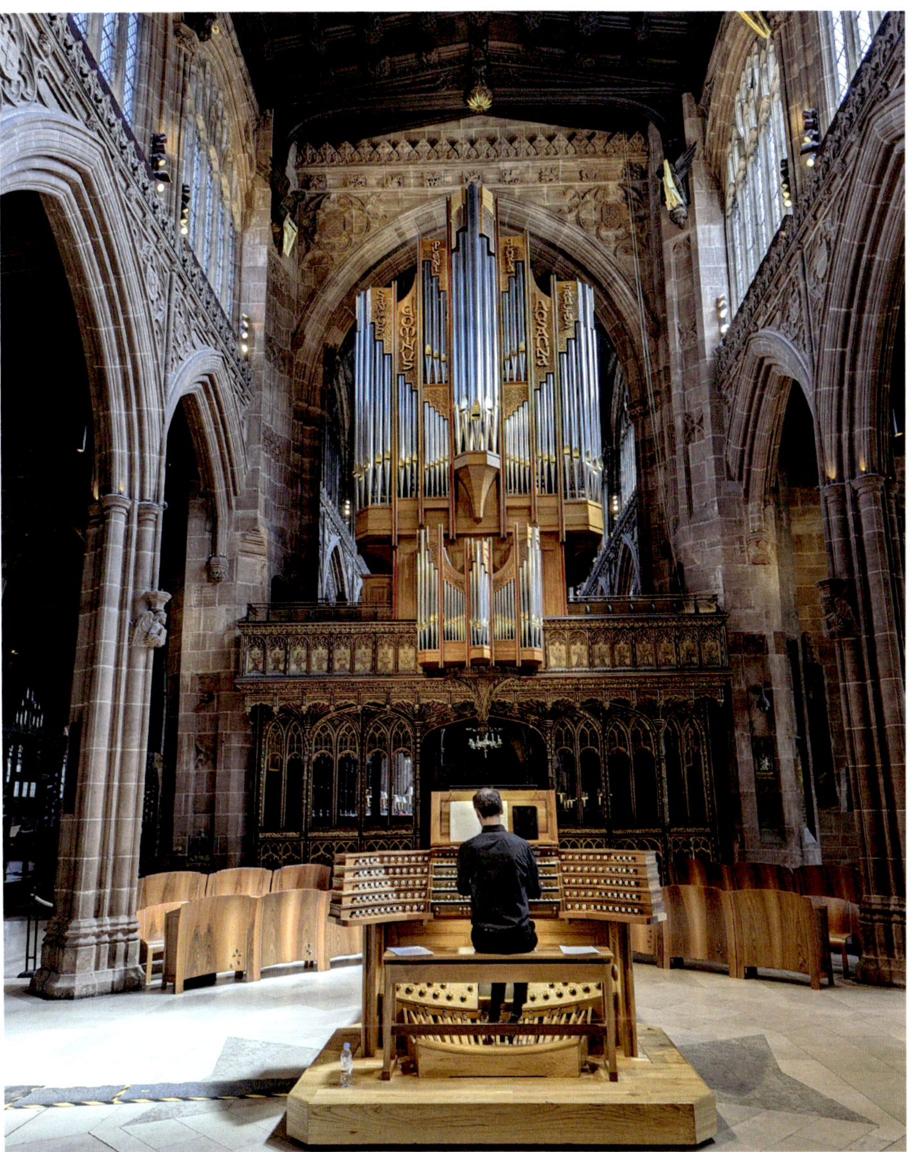

Manchester Cathedral's nave, looking east.

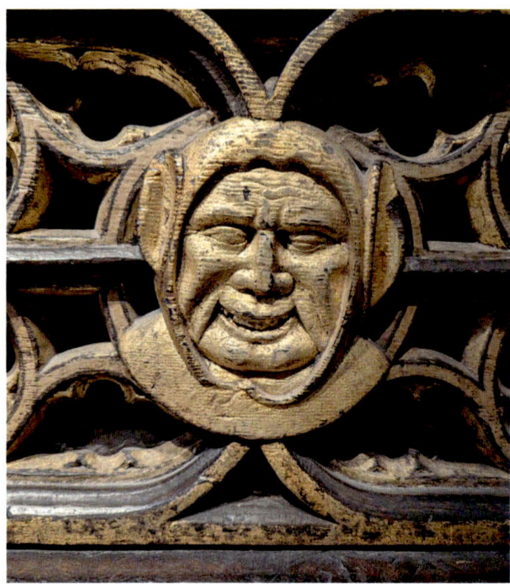

Late medieval detail of the choir screen, Manchester Cathedral.

were installed *c.* 1500–06. Their imagery is allegorical, humorous and thought provoking. Late medieval faces in wooden panelling also survive incorporated into the screen beneath the organ pipes. The misericords have been linked with the workshop of William Bromflet and the contemporary examples surviving at Ripon Cathedral (North Yorkshire) and the collegiate church that is now Beverley Minster (East Riding of Yorkshire), all dating between the 1480s and the 1520s. Our thanks for the careful restoration of the choir ceiling and for the preservation of some of the finest ecclesiastical woodwork in the stalls are in part owed to James Brown, woodworker and associate of cathedral architect Hubert Worthington, who had been engaged under Worthington's direction for other matters in the cathedral and described as 'one of the greatest craftsman in the English tradition'. The quality of the woodwork was noted by Nikolaus Pevsner, visiting several decades later.

At the north-east corner of the cathedral is the Regimental Chapel with many military flags laid up and hanging from the walls. Prior to the 'Christmas Blitz' of 1940, this chapel was an early sixteenth-century space dedicated to St John the Baptist. Part of the north wall is still original with wall brackets supported by a cast of characterful beasts with bulging eyes and leering grins. The coloured and flashed glass in the east window of the Regimental Chapel was installed in 1966 and is a design by artist Margaret Traherne titled the Fire Window. Unfortunately, this window was damaged by the explosion of an IRA bomb in 1996 and the artist returned to undertake the repair herself, having sourced replacement glass from Germany. On a bright day, I encourage you to sit and observe the wash of warm orange light cast across the chapel floor. It is a moving and peaceful experience. The church has other examples of exemplary twentieth-century stained glass by artists such as Antony Hollaway and Gerald Smith.

There is without doubt much more of interest enclosed within these modern walls than merely what would appeal only to the fanatic of Victoriana.

22. MANCHESTER, THE HOLY NAME OF JESUS

The Roman Catholic church of the Holy Name of Jesus on Oxford Road is the only Grade I listed Roman Catholic church in Manchester. It was built between 1869 and 1871 to designs by Joseph Aloysius Hansom and his son Joseph Stanislaus Hansom, but was not finally complete until 1928 under the care of architect Adrian Gilbert Scott, who designed an octagonal top to sit upon Hansom's broad west tower. Hansom's building is one of several enormous Victorian buildings facing Oxford Road and now subsumed within the expansive campus of the University of Manchester. When viewed from Ackers Street or Portsmouth Street, the church is a French cathedral in miniature. Flying buttresses

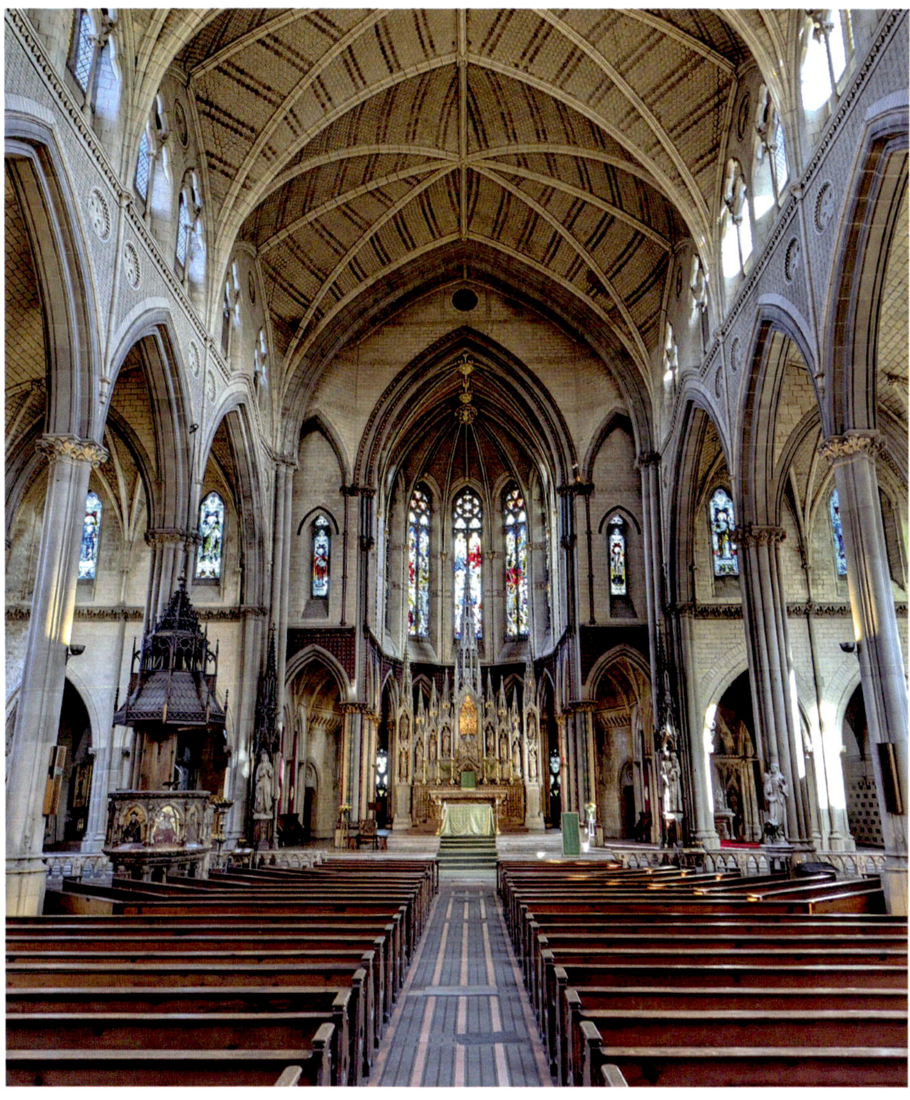

Interior of the Holy Name of Jesus Church, Manchester, looking east.

sweep around the north and south sides of the nave where they terminate against two broad transepts, from which rise two turrets to denote where the nave ends and the chancel begins. The elevation here is a thing of beauty. Flying buttresses separate bays between which are beautifully traceried, two-light windows with cusped geometric design, before they sink into the roof of the ambulatory which circumambulates the high altar.

Joseph Aloysius Hansom was born a Roman Catholic in York (North Yorkshire) in 1803 and throughout his illustrious career built numerous Gothic churches with accompanying presbyteries and church schools. His greatest achievement being the church dedicated to St Walburge in Preston (Lancashire), erected some twenty years before the Holy Name of Jesus church in Manchester.

Of the many highly decorative furnishings and fittings, it is the extraordinary pulpit designed by the younger Hansom in 1886 which deserves special attention. The sounding board is ornately carved in an architectural Gothic style befitting its extraordinary setting. It consists of an architectural canopy covered with faux roof slates and its own flying buttresses with pierced tracery patterns, reflecting the innumerable sequence of Gothic arcading separating the entrances to the north and south chapels and ancillary offices. The pulpit itself displays several mosaic portraits of holy figures such as Brother John Houghton, a priest of the Carthusian order and the first martyr to die as a result of the Royal Act of Supremacy in 1535; Edmund Campion, a Jesuit priest and martyr who died in England in 1581; Brother John Forest, a Franciscan Friar martyred in 1538; John Fisher, Catholic bishop and martyr who was executed in 1535; and Sir Thomas More, who was also put to death in the Henrician regime in 1535. Sir Thomas More wears a livery collar of 'S' or Esses. Sir Thomas More was depicted wearing the collar of 'S' with the Tudor rose of Henry VIII in his portrait by Hans Holbein the Younger.

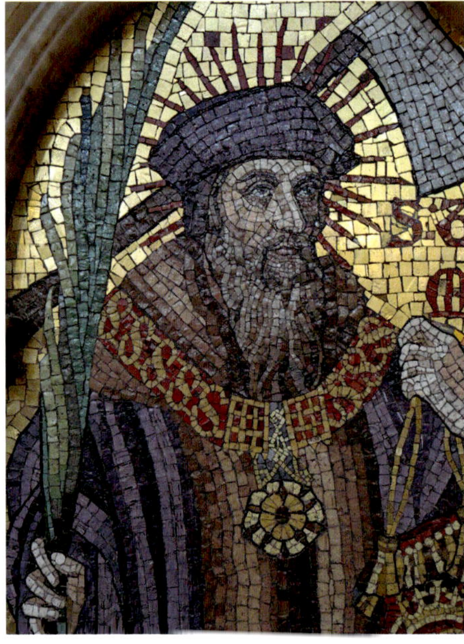

Pulpit detail of Sir Thomas More,
Holy Name of Jesus Church.

It is understood that the livery collar in the Middle Ages was intended to signify possession and ownership: that of the lord over the servant. The custom of wearing collars and neck chains as badges of office dates probably from the fourteenth century and survived until relatively modern times. The earliest description of the collar of 'S' is found in a wardrobe account of Henry Bolingbroke, Earl of Derby, in his accounts of 1391 to 1392, in which there is an entry of 'one collar of gold; with 17 letters of S made in the shape of feathers'. However, some suspect his father, John of Gaunt may have introduced the 'S'. Examples of the collar of 'S' in sculpture can be seen at Southwell Minster; York Minster's Kings Screen; St Mary's Church, Staindrop (Country Durham); St Andrew's Church, Spratton (Northamptonshire) and elsewhere.

23. MANCHESTER, ST ANN

St Ann's Square was laid out in 1720 as the first major development away from the medieval centre around the old market and medieval church. The buildings lining the square and on nearby Kings Street, through which access is gained via St Ann's Passage (a delightful, short arcade), are more consistent in style and scale with each other than the more familiar piecemeal approach to the urban development of the city centre. Construction of St Ann's church started in 1709, preceding the erection of the delightful buildings around which it is surrounded today.

St Ann's Church was founded by Lady Ann Bland (née Mosley), after whom the dedication is given, who obtained the necessary Act of Parliament in 1708 and built her church as an alternative to the high church order of service which was followed at the collegiate church in the old town at the time. Standing in St Ann's Square looking up at the building, it is important to remember you are looking at the north elevation. Access today is by the north door under the modest classical portico and stone pediment, or by the west door under the west tower. One wonders whether the tower was intended to have a small tower or cupola built on top, as numerous town churches of the eighteenth century so often did in their later years. The answer is, yes, St Ann's originally had a three-stage cupola, but this was removed in 1777 and replaced by the upper stage of the current tower we see today.

Alfred Waterhouse and his son undertook a restoration of the church in the nineteenth century which reduced the visual impact of the box pews (with original brass name plates), added new stained-glass windows and rearranged the choir in the small apsidal chancel; however, it has been noted that the interventions were restrained and sensitive. An altar and reredos were added with an intricate carved design with cherubs in the panelling above the altar, taking influence from the work of Grinling Gibbons. Waterhouse did not remove the interior galleries or contemporary furnishings and fittings, choosing to retain them and the character of the Georgian church. The three-decker pulpit was only slightly altered, with the intention chiefly to stabilise it in position. Annibale Carracci's painting *Descent from the Cross* which once hung in St Peter's Church, demolished in 1907, is now on display in St Ann's Church.

The stained glass is all at eyeline in the nave aisles and all very beautiful. Of particular interest and something of a rarity is a window of painted glass across

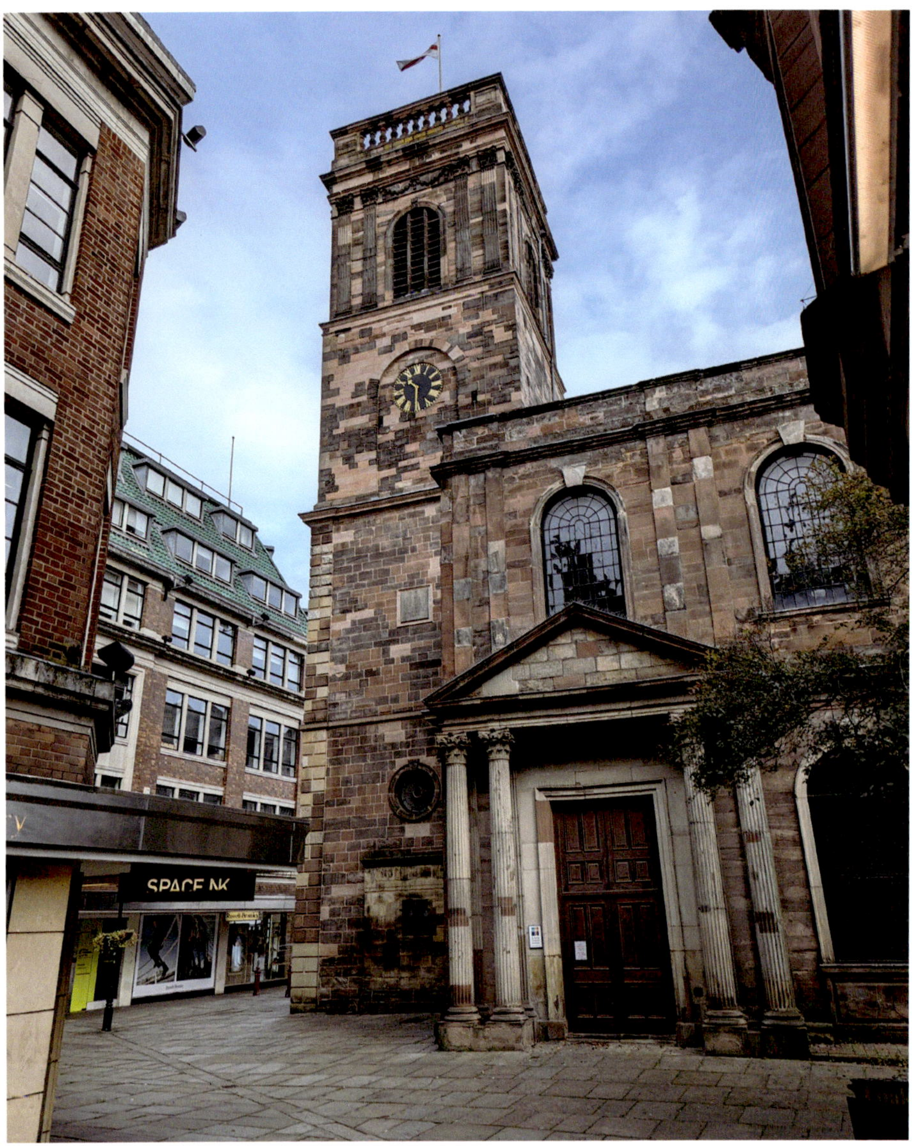

St Ann's, Manchester.

three lights depicting St John, St Peter and St Matthew, made in 1769 by William Peckitt of York (North Yorkshire). This was originally for the east window of St John's Church on Byrom Street, Deansgate, now demolished and relocated here by York Glaziers Trust 1981. With notable works in the south transept of York Minster, parish churches and stately homes, Peckitt was a prolific glazier of his time; a time when the production of stained and painted glass was not widely practised.

In June 1996, the Irish Republican Army (IRA) detonated a 3,300-lb bomb on Corporation Street, roughly half a mile from St Ann's Church. It was the largest

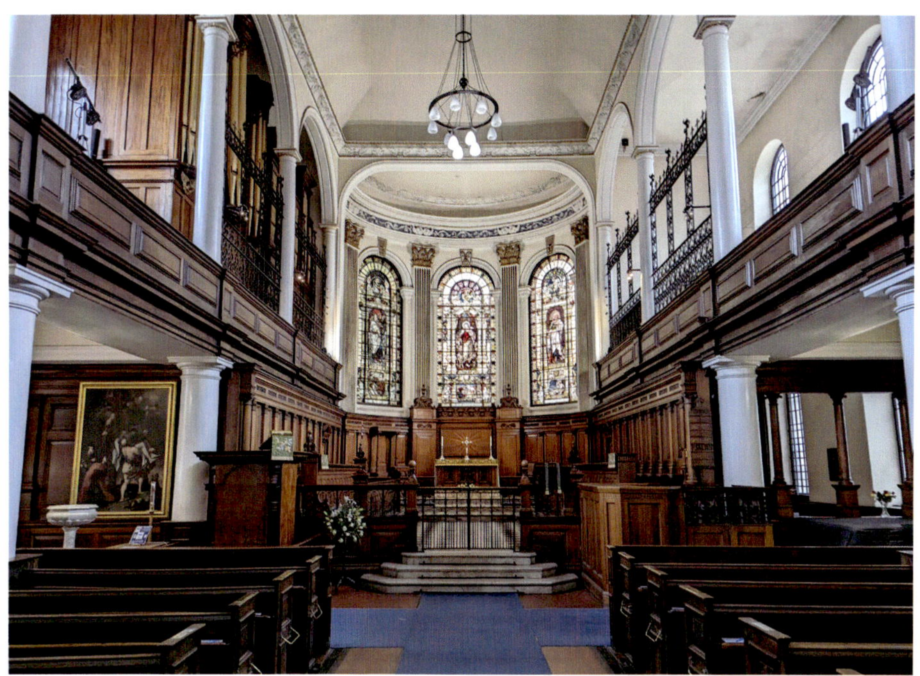

Above: Interior of St Ann's, looking east.

Right: William Peckitt window, St Ann's.

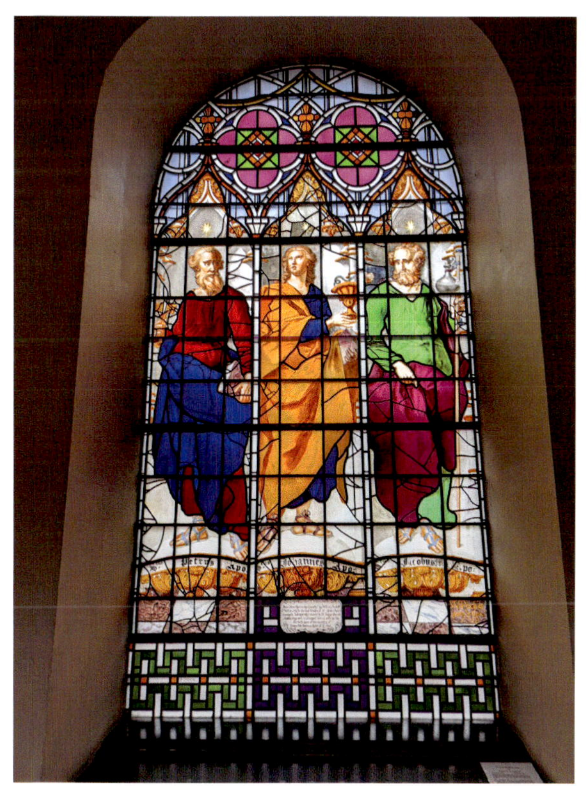

bomb to be detonated since the Second World War. The explosion was so vast that the city centre lost around 40 per cent of its retail and office space, surging Manchester City Council's longstanding aspiration to 'reinvent' the city centre. The impact of the blast damaged some stained-glass windows in both St Ann's Church and Manchester Cathedral. One window in the church here has a small brass plaque commemorating its restoration after this incident, and in memory of a couple who were married in St Ann's in 1946.

24. MANCHESTER, ST AUGUSTINE

There are a handful of modernist churches in Greater Manchester of variable merit, but none are quite so provocative as St Augustine's on Grosvenor Square, which has remained largely unaltered, located in the heart of what is now Manchester Metropolitan University. A squat building faced with dark brown brick and constructed of seemingly modular forms, this unassuming church was built between 1966 and 1986 to designs by architects Desmond Williams and Associates, with money from the War Damage Commission. The square, load-bearing exterior only deviates from the use of straight line by the inclusion of a large ceramic plate with a star and mitre by artist Robert Brumby. A small taste for what may be seen inside.

The interior is a little less severe than the entrance overlooking Grosvenor Square. Internal brick piers contain thin lights of coloured glass by renowned ecclesiastical glaziers James Powell & Sons, or Whitefriars Glass, but they do not illuminate the interior. A raked ceiling draws the eye towards an enormous

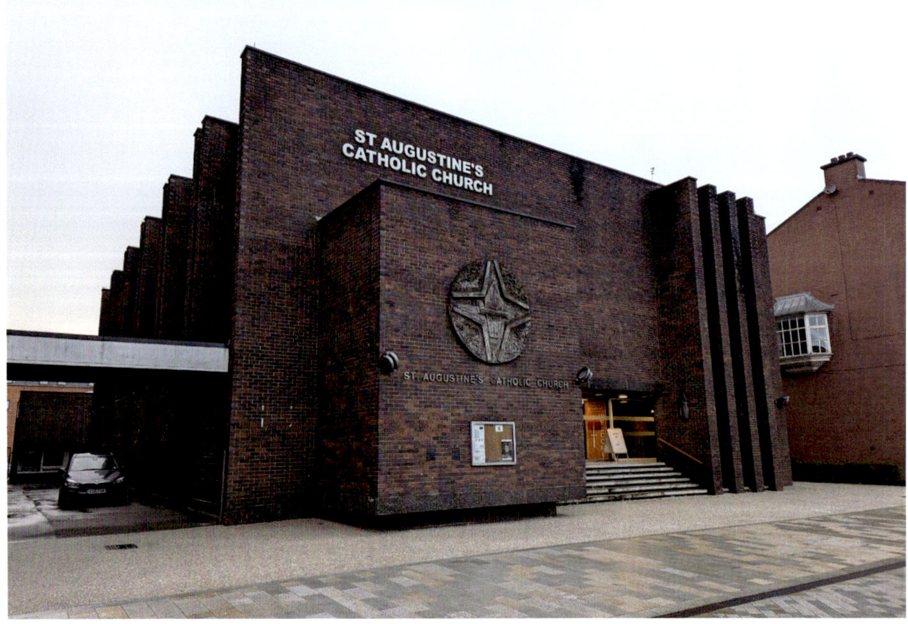

St Augustine's, Manchester.

and striking artwork behind the high altar which commands the interior. *Christ Sitting in Majesty Over Creation* is the work of artist Robert Brumby. It is simply astonishing. Thousands of shards of small clay tile, concrete, ceramic and metal create great swirling forms around a central figure of Christ with his arms outstretched. At the centre of two of these swirling circular forms are small panels depicting the Holy Spirit and a chalice. Notice the three-dimensional materiality of the sculpture and how it is downlit to great effect. It must have been tempting to spotlight this larger-than-life artwork, which might have washed out the full impact of its rough texture. Instead, a faint blue light is cast over the head of the figure and gradually fades out, creating a seamless transition from shadow into the warm, earthy highlights of tile and ceramic.

Christ Sitting in Majesty Over Creation is somewhat reminiscent of works by artists Jacob Epstein and Elizabeth Frink. It is not implausible that Epstein's sculpture *Victory over the Devil* at Coventry Cathedral was an inspiration here. At one time in his career, Robert Brumby was in charge of ceramics at York School of Art between 1960 and 1967. His other ecclesiastical commissions include *Christ in Majesty and Holy Family Group* for the Church of the Holy Family in Pontefract, a Crucifixion for Hull University Catholic Chaplaincy, and a Madonna and Child for the Lady Chapel in Liverpool Cathedral.

St Augustine's owes a great deal to the Robert Brumby and Desmond Williams and Associates, who appear to have worked collaboratively to create a unified scheme of furnishings and fittings, with Brumby also designing holy water stoups,

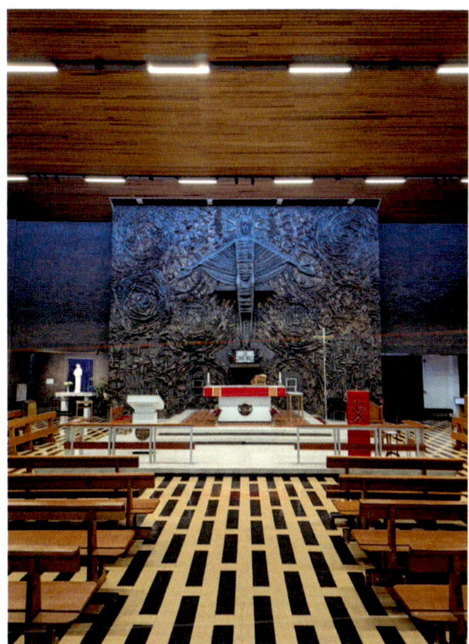
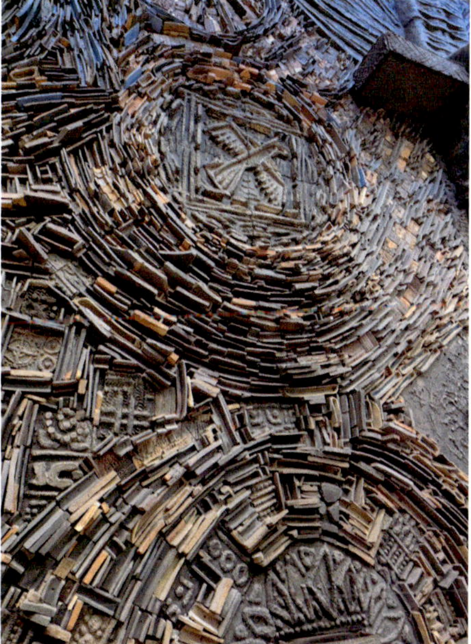

Above left: Robert Brumby's *Christ Sitting in Majesty Over Creation* at St Augustine's, Manchester.

Above right: Detail of Brumby's mural, St Augustine's.

brackets light fittings, and a plain stone font with a complimentary, flat metal cover. He also designed the high altar table and the Stations of the Cross sculptures and a memorial plaque commemorating the earlier parish church which this replaced after it was destroyed in the Second World War.

25. MANCHESTER, ST PETER'S CROSS

It is important to share the story of one of Manchester's greatest lost churches and how the public setting of its former site has quite extensively changed in the past 200 years. So many of central Manchester's historic churches have been lost to demolition as the city centre has been renewed, but one surviving landmark tells a fascinating story and is often passed by, unknown to so many.

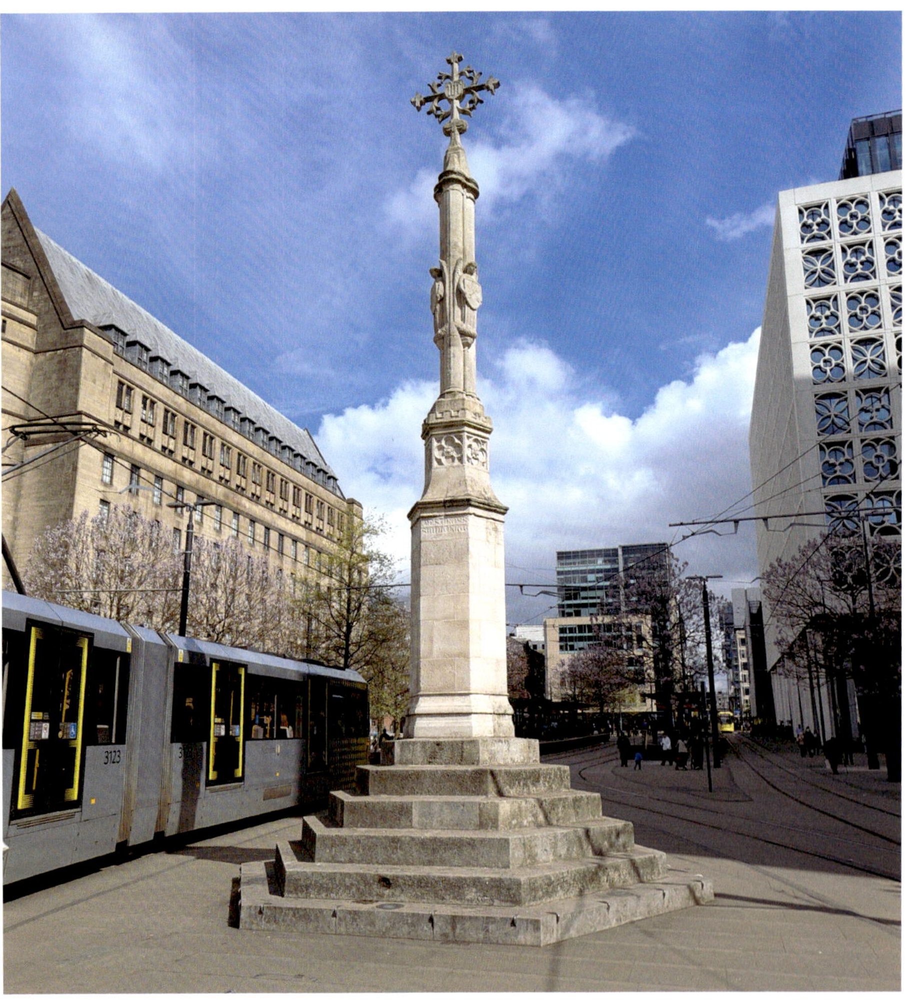

St Peter's Cross, Manchester.

When architect James Wyatt's church dedicated to St Peter standing in St Peter's Square was demolished in 1907, the site was marked by a Gothic-style cross carved from Portland stone and designed by architect Temple Moore. The cross is said to have been installed over the area where the high altar stood in the former neoclassical church. The cross stands on a hexagonal plinth and is adorned with angels bearing the emblem of St Peter, the cross keys.

Wyatt's austere and bulky church was built in 1794, with a later tower added by Francis Goodwin in 1824 and was originally surrounded by open fields. It is unfathomable nowadays to think of its relatively rural setting and that the church witnessed the rapid expansion of the Victorian city which built up around the existing square. From 1924 a cenotaph monument designed by Edwin Lutyens was located on the site of the lost church next to the St Peter's Cross with a small garden. In 2014 the cenotaph was relocated due to Manchester City Council's major redevelopment of St Peter's Square, which focused on the expansion of the Metrolink stop that now dominates the area.

It has been said that when Wyatt's church was demolished some burial vaults were sealed over, and when the archaeologists were on site for the development at the new Metrolink site, a crypt was discovered. This contained several artefacts from the graves of the deceased of late Georgian Manchester. Metrolink resealed the burial vaults and covered the crypt with 750 tonnes of concrete to protect it for the future.

Temple Moore's memorial cross, however, has not moved and stands today on an island either side of the tram lines with the outline of the ground plan of the demolished church marked out in subtle paving details.

26. MARPLE, ALL SAINTS

A full circle ring of eight church bells have often been heard to ring out from Marple, but not from the parish church as one might expect. If the reader approaches All Saints' Churchyard uphill from the town centre, walking past the Ring O' Bells pub, they will at first be greeted with the sight of a free-standing church tower which was once part of a large Georgian Chapel built to replace a timber-framed chapel dating to the 16th century that had been severely damaged during a storm in 1804. The detached tower is adjacent to a late Victorian church on the same site designed by architects James Medland Taylor and Henry Taylor in 1880 which is today an active place of worship. In front of the tower facing Church Street is also an old stable, hearse house and primitive lychgate which all served the Georgian chapel.

For many years both churches were used for services, but over time the Georgian chapel fell out of favour with its congregation, who favoured the more modern Victorian church a stone's throw away. By 1964 the chapel had become dangerous, and action was taken to demolish the preaching box-style nave and small chancel but to leave the bell tower intact. James Medland Taylor and Henry Taylor had actually omitted a bell tower from their design for the new church in 1880 as a cost-saving decision to retain the detached tower of the Georgian chapel. In 1964 the original six bells were returned with two additional bells cast by Taylors of

Loughborough and the full ring of eight was rehung. At the same time a new ground-floor ringing chamber was constructed and the tower strengthened.

Monuments from the old church are preserved inside the new ringing chamber and one is notable as the memorial to the Georgian church's principal patron, Samuel Oldknow. The Georgian tower is well maintained and certainly a unique approach to preserving a structure designed specifically for the purpose of upholding the great national tradition of English change ringing. The Marple bell-ringers keep the bells sounding out across the town.

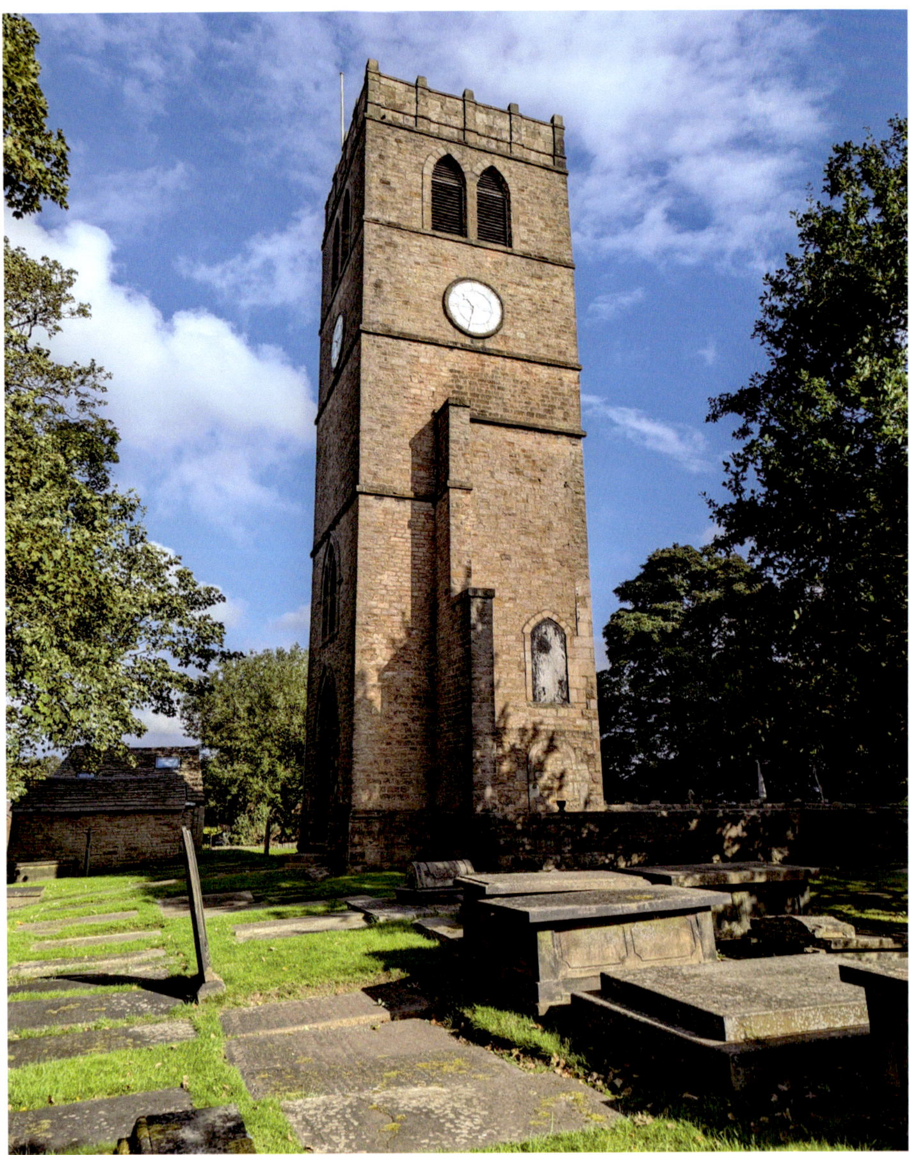

All Saints' Church, Marple.

27. LOW MARPLE, ST MARTIN

Sitting on a steep bank looking down towards the village of Low Marple is St Martin's Church. The road to the church leads down to a settlement, bridging both banks of the River Goyt, all much closer to Stockport than it is to Manchester. Conveniently located mere yards from the ticket office at Marple railway station serving the Hope Valley Line, St Martin's Church was in fact built only a few years after this railway station opened.

St Martin's is a small and unassuming village church built in the Arts and Crafts style, modest in character, constructed of rough stone ashlar with a simple half-timber south porch, but boasting an interior of artistic and architectural merit well above any other Arts and Crafts church in Greater Manchester. It was designed by eminent architect J. D. Sedding between 1869 and 1870. Construction was piecemeal, with a north aisle and north chapel added later by Henry Wilson in 1895–96 and again in 1909.

Of the various spaces within the handsome interior, those of greatest artistic interest are contained to the north aisle. Facing the south door is the tremendous St Christopher Chapel, which is dominated by a Renaissance-style plaster sculpture quite clearly inspired by Michelangelo. The St Christopher sculpture was recently cleaned by conservator Veronika Viková. The sculpture is the work of architect and craftsman Henry Wilson, who succeeded J. D. Sedding after his death in the ongoing embellishment of the church. Wilson's sculpture of St Christopher was

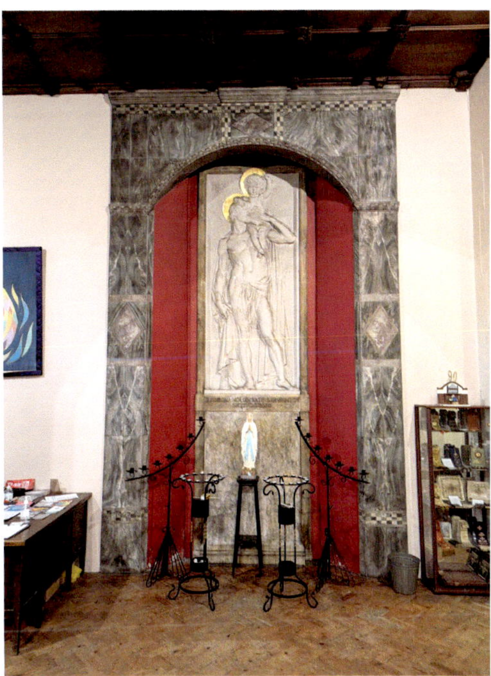 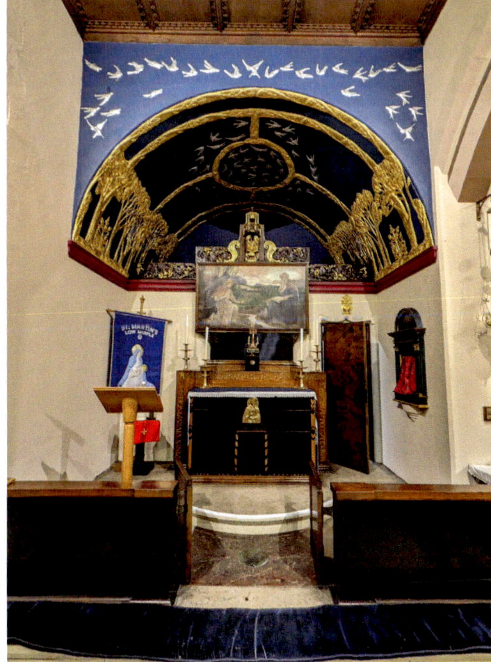

Above left: St Christopher Chapel at St Martin's, Low Marple.

Above right: Lady Chapel at St Martin's.

installed in 1909 as a memorial to Miss Maria Ann Hudson, who was heavily involved in the foundation of St Martin's Church. The larger-than-life sculpture faces you as you enter the church by the south entrance, a setting with historical precedence going back to medieval schemes for the decoration of English parish churches, where an image of St Christopher was often painted on the north wall in this spot where they could be easily seen. It was thought that seeing this image as entered church would in some way protect the beholder from dying an evil death on the same day.

In the same part of the church there is an unusual barrel vault above the altar in the Lady Chapel at the east end of the north aisle, designed by Christopher Wall with gesso-work on the vault of the small apse. Gilded trees and white doves surround the ribs lining the interior of the blue vault, giving depth to this very distinct and separate alcove containing a small altar.

28. MIDDLETON, ST LEONARD

Before the Industrial Revolution arrived in Middleton, St Leonard's Square, which had the medieval parish church at its heart, was the focal point of the old town settled on a ridge towards Rochdale. A steep incline on approach to the church from the east rises to look out upon suburban views of Greater Manchester towards Chadderton and Oldham.

St Leonard's is one of the most impressive medieval parish churches in Greater Manchester. Hundreds of ledger stones and old headstones form a series of extensive paved areas and paths around the churchyard, and much time can be spent observing the seventeenth- and eighteenth-century epitaphs and 'memento mori' upon them. Some of the flat stones serve as burial records for several generations of the same family, noting initials and dates of death in changing stylised script by the stonemason.

Although the exterior pale sandstone masonry is in some places badly weathered, the south elevation of the church is nevertheless the most rewarding. The south porch, lower stone stages of the west tower and south arcade date from 1412 for Thomas Langley, Dean of York, Bishop of Durham, twice Lord Chancellor to three successive English kings. The west tower was topped with a unique weather-boarded belfry stage in around 1667, when it is known that new bells were hung, making it quite individual in Greater Manchester. Leeds-born antiquarian and historian Ralph Thoresby once described the wooden top as appearing to be more appropriate for a 'dovecot' than a church. In spite of significant stone deterioration, the embattled late medieval south porch still shows enough of its original ornate detailing to impress, although it is regrettable that the inscription is illegible.

St Leonard's built history is both complex and fascinating. The vestry in the south-east corner was constructed in 1662. Architect George G. Pace constructed a new north porch and vestries between 1957 and 1960. But much of the existing fabric is a hodgepodge of earlier building phases. The main point of interest is the reuse of architectural masonry which once formed a twelfth-century round arch but now makes up three arched orders of a pointed tower arch constructed

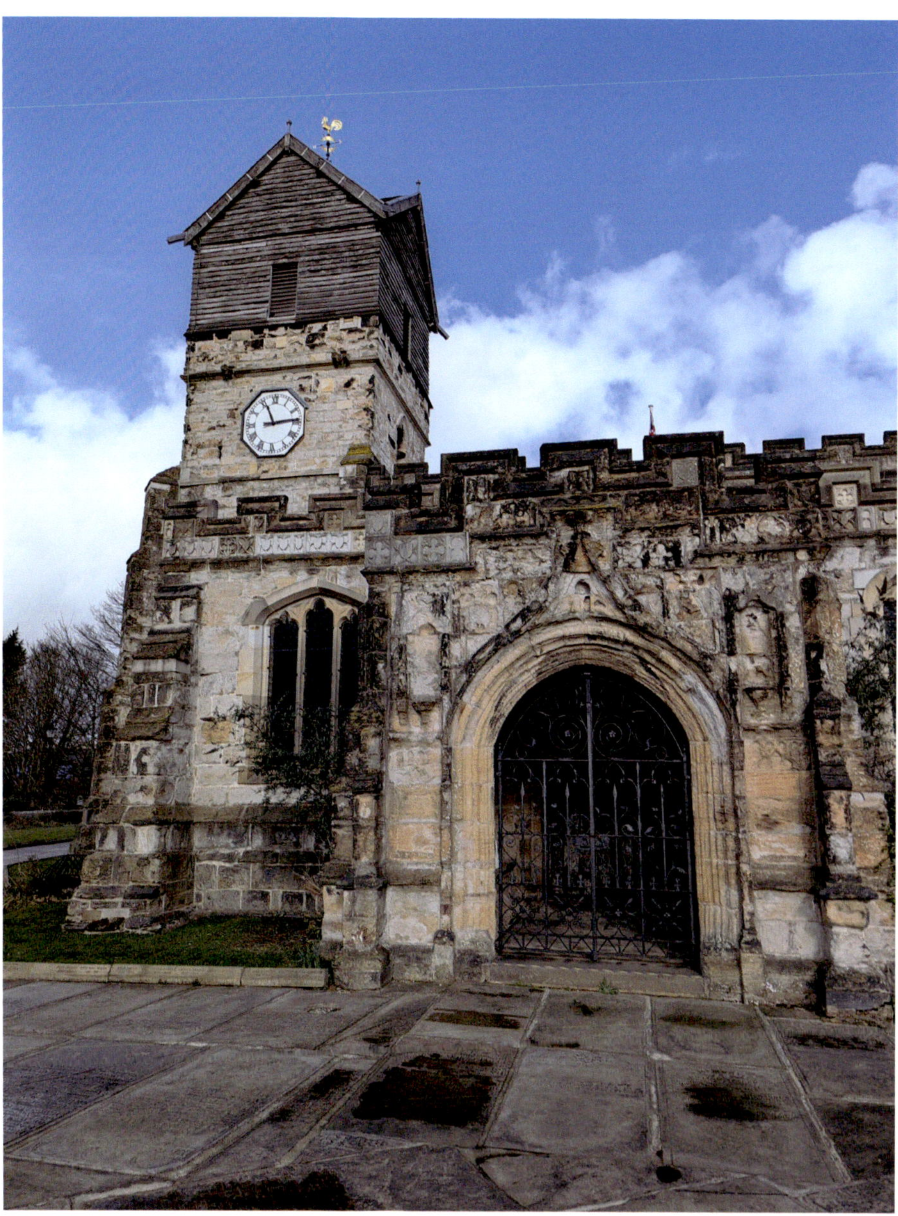

St Leonard's, Middleton.

in 1412, containing chevon voussoirs for the most part with some more straightforward mouldings. Various scalloped carved ornamentation and other patterns decorate the capitals. It has been suggested by architectural historian Dr James Cameron that Thomas Langley had a reverence for Romanesque building fabric. Langley was buried against the former west door of the Galilee Chapel in Durham Cathedral (County Durham), a twelfth-century structure

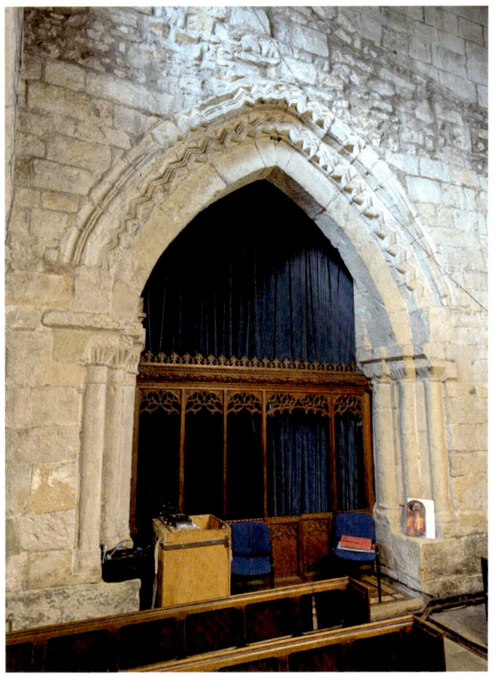

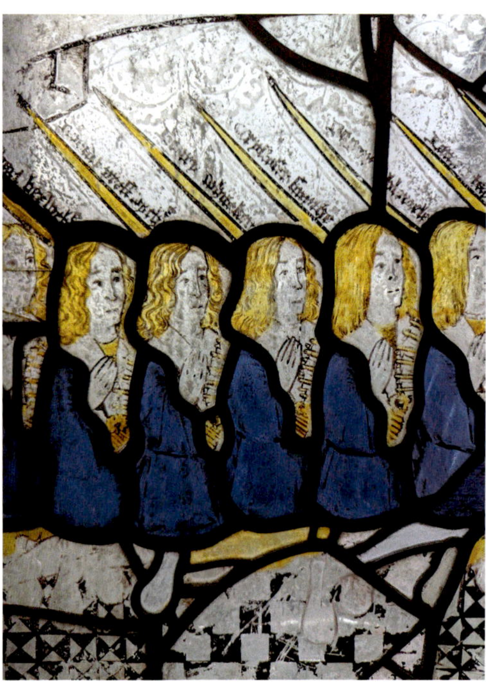

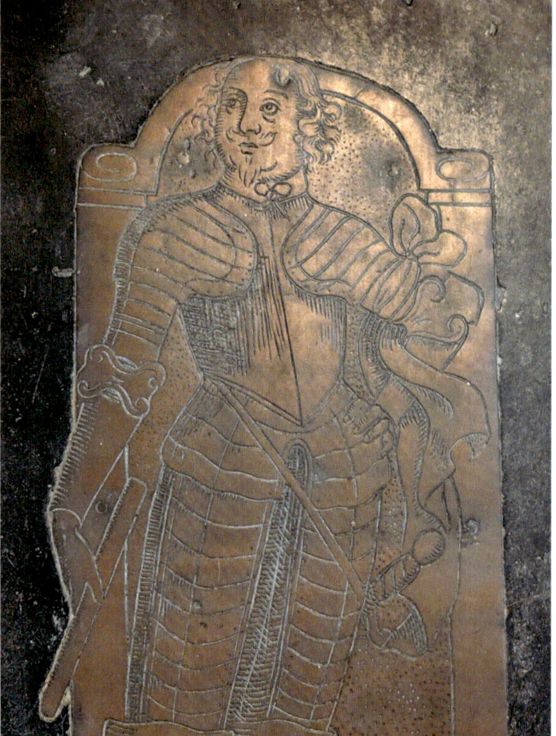

Above left: Interior tower arch,
St Leonard's.

Above right: Detail of archers in the
Flodden Window, St Leonard's.

Left: Ralph Assheton memorial brass,
St Leonard's.

consolidated during Langley's time as Bishop of Durham. St Leonard's was once again partially rebuilt, this time in 1524 by Richard Assheton, brother of Revd Edmund Assheton, who is one of a series of local worthies represented in brass in front of the high altar. Richard Assheton is also responsible for the installation of a nationally significant stained-glass window which could have been lost were it not for the intervention of Revd Richard Durnford in the nineteenth century, who recognised its subject and age and went to great lengths to reassemble what was left of it and install the remains in a two light south window in the chancel. 'The Flodden Window' was installed in 1515 and commemorates the victory over Scottish invaders at the Battle of Flodden in September 1513. This was a victory that prompted the subsequent rebuilding of St Leonard's Church. The window depicts seventeen Middleton archers, including Richard Assheton himself as their leader. They are named individually in the window and the tops of their longbows can be seen beside them.

The collection of monumental brasses here is the finest and most extensive in Greater Manchester. Grouped together in the floor of the chancel and not in their original locations are memorial depictions of clergy and members of notable noble families, all shown wearing the appropriate costume of their period. The most impressive is that commemorating Ralph Assheton, whose Parliamentary uniform and boots are particularly eye-catching and flamboyant. In 2004, the brass of the aforementioned Revd Edmund Assheton, who died in 1522, was removed for conservation and on inspection was found to be palimpsest. A palimpsest is a monumental brass which has been recycled with details of an earlier brass monument on the reverse. In this instance it is thought that the inscription and image on the reverse could be dated to the early fourteenth century, making it one of the earliest known monumental brasses in the country.

29. MIDDLETON, ST MICHAEL

There are several local architects named in this book who appear more than once, having worked across Lancashire and what we consider to be Greater Manchester today. Sharpe, Paley and Austin is one such practice, although in the case of St Michael's Church in Middleton, the practice was then simply Paley and Austin (more information in Geoff Brandwood's seminal book *The Architecture of Sharpe, Paley and Austin*, published in 2012). In designing new churches, the firm became well known for a dominant Perpendicular Gothic style. St Michael's is no exception. Constructed between 1901 and 1930, replacing an earlier church dating back to 1839. Initially, only the east end and the first bay of the nave were built. The nave was completed in 1911 and the detached north-west tower was added between 1926 and 1931. The tower is reminiscent of Perpendicular Gothic towers dating back to the late medieval period. The grey stone structure calls to mind Abbot Huby's tower of 1526 at Fountains Abbey (North Yorkshire).

The design for the rest of this large church includes a four-bay nave with a clerestory, north and south aisles, a chancel with a side chapel, vestry, and organ

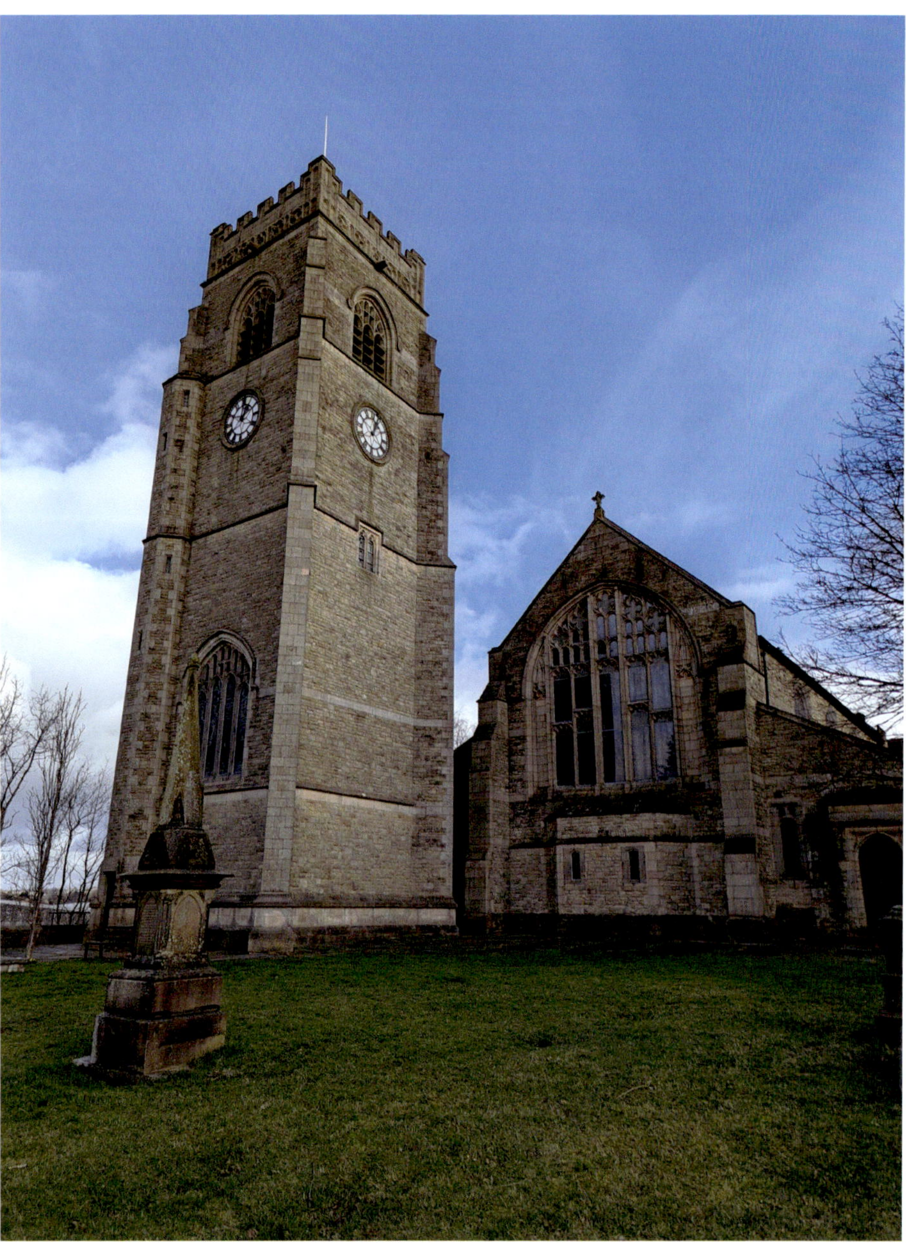

St Michael's, Middleton.

chamber. The north-west tower is a Gothic beacon on this elevated site looking across to the ancient parish church dedicated to St Leonard. It consists of four stages, angle buttresses, an octagonal stair turret, a belfry stage and a castellated parapet. Inside, the arcades are carried on octagonal piers, and most of the stained glass is by the firm Shrigley and Hunt.

30. OLDHAM PARISH CHURCH (ST MARY AND ST PETER)

Unlike Rochdale, Oldham was a small hamlet in the Middle Ages with a medieval parish church which has now entirely disappeared after it was demolished in 1827. Nothing of the medieval parish church remains above ground save for two old parish chests probably dating from the fifteenth and sixteenth centuries, but in the crypt it is possible to see some evidence confirming the presence of a medieval church, most notably by a small coffin now set into a wall of an unused burial plot. Although not of the original church, an eighteenth-century weathercock

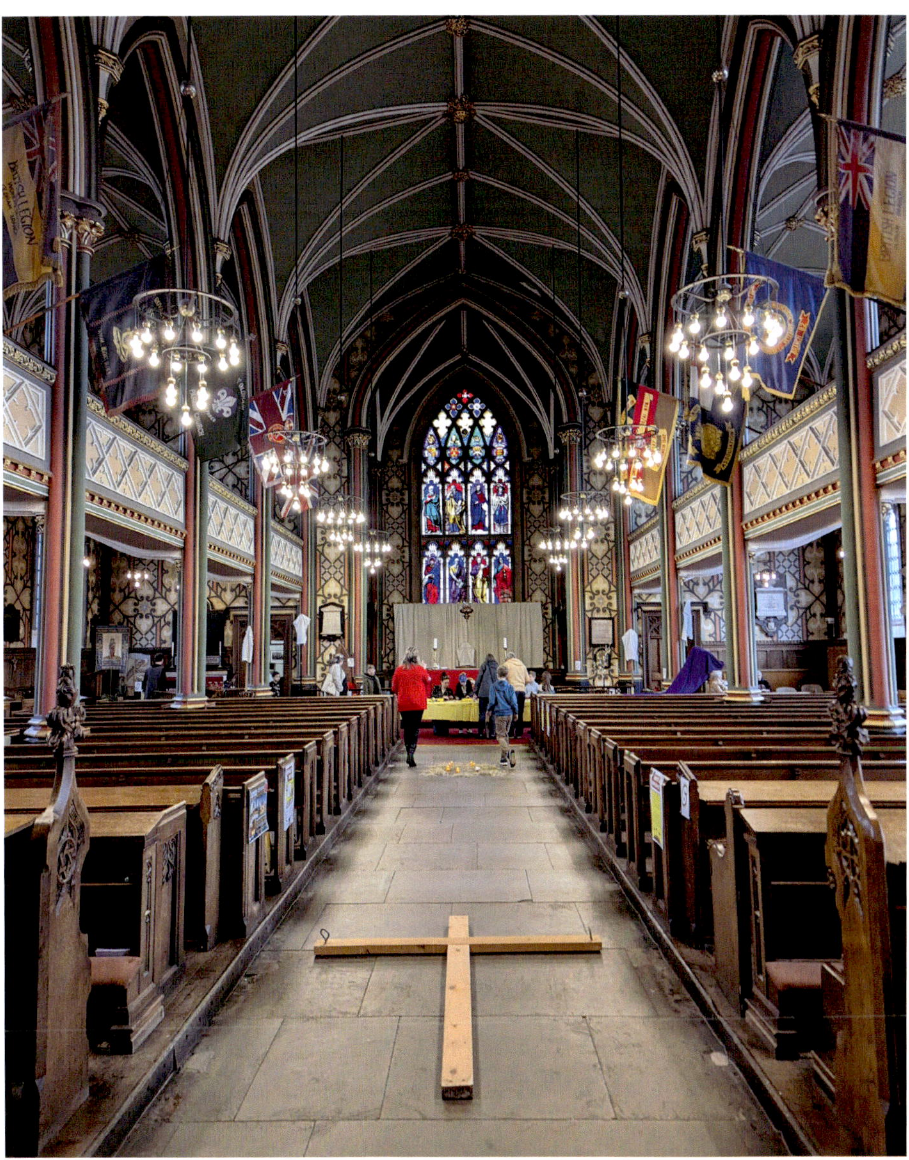

Interior of Oldham Parish Church, looking east.

shown on the top of the tower in antiquarian drawings of the old church prior to demolition is now stored behind the main entrance door to the south. It is an impressive example of folk art and a pleasing, handmade, weatherbeaten object.

The church is the jewel of a former mill town built on a prominent hillside overlooking much of Greater Manchester. The present church was designed by architect Richard Lane after his design submitted for a competition in 1824 was selected over submissions from other prolific architects of the day such as Charles Barry, Matthew Habershon and Francis Goodwin. Designs for Barry's church are kept in the vestry, and it is said that the Oldham locals at the time were so unsatisfied with Barry's proposal that they opposed it being built, despite the fact it was the preferred design of the bishop.

Lane's church is eccentrically decorated, although it is not an original scheme. The slender nave arcades separating the wide aisles from the central worship space are all painted in bright colours resembling a repeated wallpaper pattern. The scheme is purported to be inspired by a medieval design and although it is in that vague style, it actually feels to be more idiosyncratic rather than inspired by historical precedent. Each surface of the interior is painted in reds and greens. This was all the result of a decorative scheme by architect Stephen Dykes Bower in 1975.

St Mary's is unique in Greater Manchester for making its extensive crypt almost entirely accessible to the public when they host guided tours. The crypt

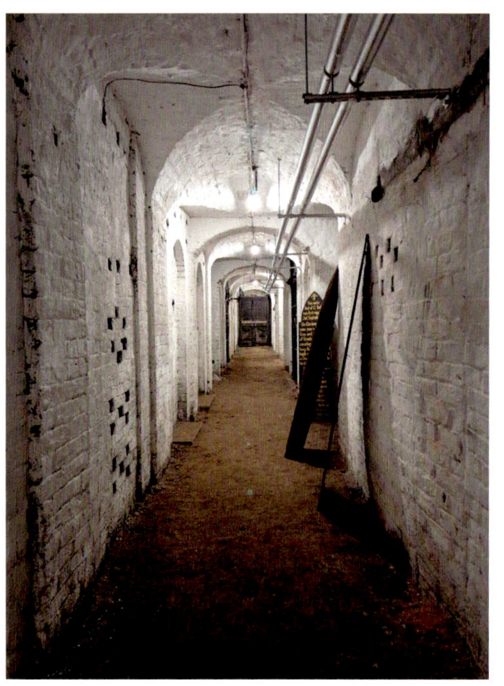

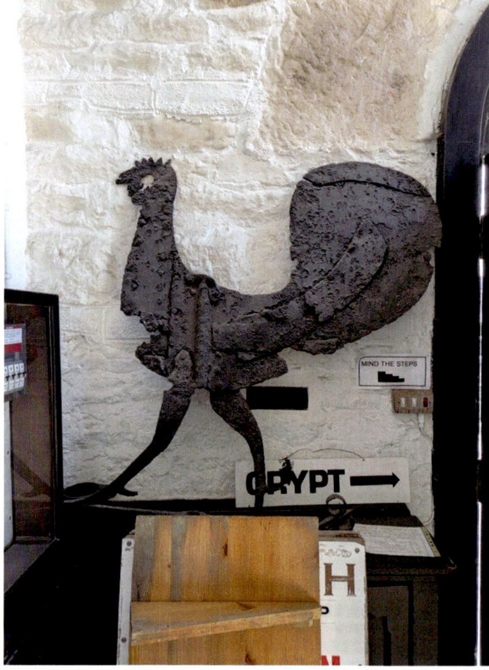

Above left: The crypt at Oldham Parish Church.

Above right: The old weathercock, Oldham

is unusually large and deliberately so as it was intended that income from selling burial space here would offset overspending on the building of the new church above ground. There are eighty-four vaults in total, of which only a mere fraction have been filled. They were generally purchased by wealthy families, and the coffins therein are visibly expensive objects with metal plates, some behind heavy cast-iron gates. When a vault was filled it was generally bricked up and sealed, with small apertures to allow a small viewpoint into each chamber, but these brick partitions could be taken down if a new coffin was to be placed inside. It is easy to get lost in the winding subterranean corridors, but on the north side of the central passageway is the coffin containing the bones of the 'Oldham Giant', Joseph Scholes. Scholes was something of a local celebrity in his day. He was a hatter by trade before periods working in the military and as governor of an Oldham workhouse. He was born in 1758 and died in 1814. It is said that he weighed over 37 stone and was over 6 feet in height. His coffin, which is visible in its burial vault today, measures 6.5 by 3 yards and required twelve men to carry in for his funeral.

31. PRESTWICH, ST MARY

The parish of Prestwich-cum-Oldham was once one of the largest parishes in England and was in the diocese of Lichfield until 1541. According to some sources, the old parish spanned 21,625 acres and its population exceeded 94,000 in 1851, a number which gradually declined in later years. For a period of time, the parish church dedicated to St Mary in Prestwich was the principal church where residents of the towns and villages within the area travelled far and wide to attend. This is testament to its substantial churchyard, uncommonly large by any standard, spanning almost 8 acres in size with a total of twenty-four separately listed monuments, grave slabs, a hearse house, mounting block and war memorial cross.

St Mary's Church is built in red sandstone and has a fine, battlemented fifteenth-century west tower with sixteenth-century nave and aisles. To approach the churchyard by the appropriately named Church Lane and Church Inn, the elevation of the church is distinctly medieval. But to then walk around to the east side of the building, it becomes apparent how much was renewed and added in the nineteenth century. The predominant change was a substantial reordering and rebuilding in 1888 and 1889 by Austin & Paley, although inside this did not detract from the character of this ancient building.

Inside, the nave ceiling is a triumph and one of several late medieval ceilings in the Greater Manchester area. Although it is not quite late medieval, in fact, nor the greatest in splendour, but of overall good quality sixteenth-century woodwork. Some sources suggest the foliate pattern ceiling bosses could date it to the fifteenth century. The candelabra which hangs in the central aisle of the nave is much like the one in St Mary's, Deane, near Oldham, and dates from the eighteenth century. It is topped with an eagle and child, a symbol taken from the emblem of the Earl of Derby who owned land in the parish at the time of its donation to the church.

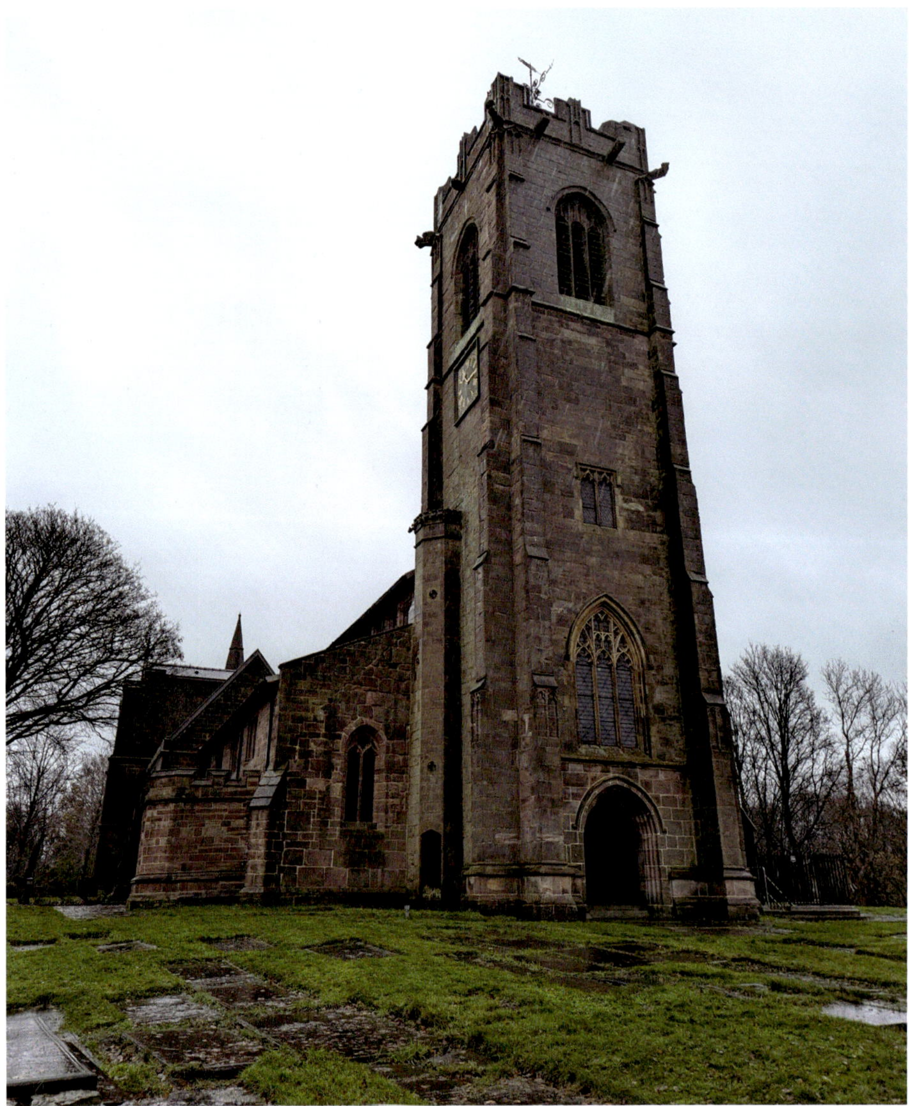

St Mary's, Prestwich.

The Leyer Chapel is an interesting space with a private staircase at its east end to an upper level which is no longer present. The relationship of the Lee family, who once occupied this private chapel, may have been at odds with other users of the building. The extension of the church east of the Leyer Chapel in 1874 was undertaken with the consent of the owners of the Leyer Chapel by promise by the then patron, rector, churchwardens and parishioners that no gallery, organ, musical instrument or other objectionable structure should be placed therein, and that if this promise was breached then it would be permitted for a partition wall to be built, separating the chapel from the extension.

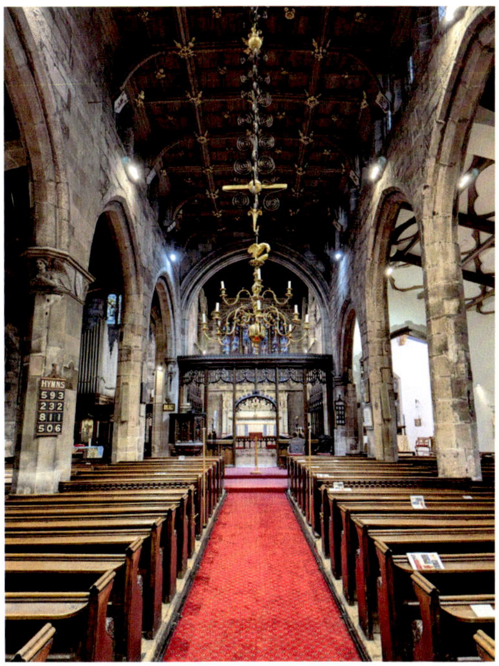

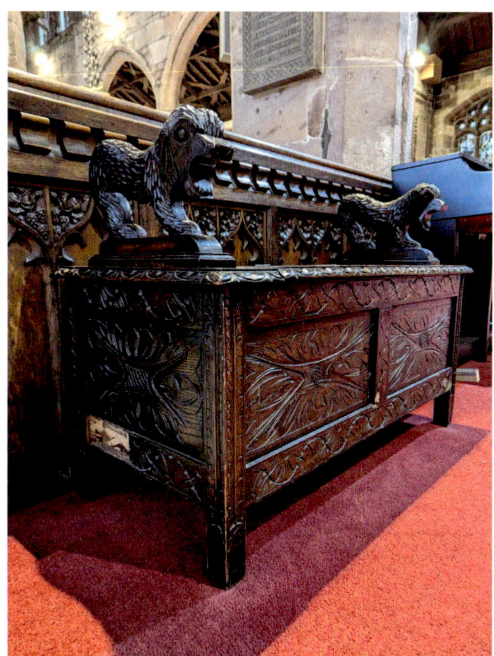

Above left: Interior of St Mary's, looking east.

Above right: Parish chest, St Mary's, Prestwich.

Otherwise, most of the fittings and furnishings, including the nave pews, chancel screen, organ casement, polychromatic marble floor in the chancel, are late Victorian, as well as brightly coloured stained glass by glaziers Clayton & Bell and Shrigley and Hunt of Lancaster.

32. RADCLIFFE, ST MARY

St Mary's is one of Greater Manchester's medieval church buildings in a most picturesque setting forming part of an unusual cluster of ancient structures including a nearby tithe barn and medieval ruin known as the Radcliffe Tower, which formed part of a moated manor house rebuilt in 1403 by James de Radcliffe, lord of the manor of Radcliffe. The church was dedicated to both St Mary and St Bartholomew until 1991 when several parishes merged and the present name and dedication was adopted.

The oldest-surviving parts of the church are the chancel arch and fifteenth-century nave and nave arcades. But much of what can be seen today changed in more recent years. The church underwent substantial development from the seventeenth century to the nineteenth century. The west tower was rebuilt and altered in the fifteenth century and then again in the seventeenth century, latterly under the guidance of Revd Charles Beswick, who was rector from 1661 to 1697. A date stone in the west façade above the west door bears his name and the date 1665.

The church was badly affected by the Boxing Day floods of 2015. St Mary's was filled with water to waist height when the River Irwell flooded and many of the church's historic furnishings, fittings and treasures, including an incised memorial slab dating to 1410, were displaced or covered with dirty water for several days. An extensive restoration and clearing of the interior was promptly underway when access to the building was possible two days later.

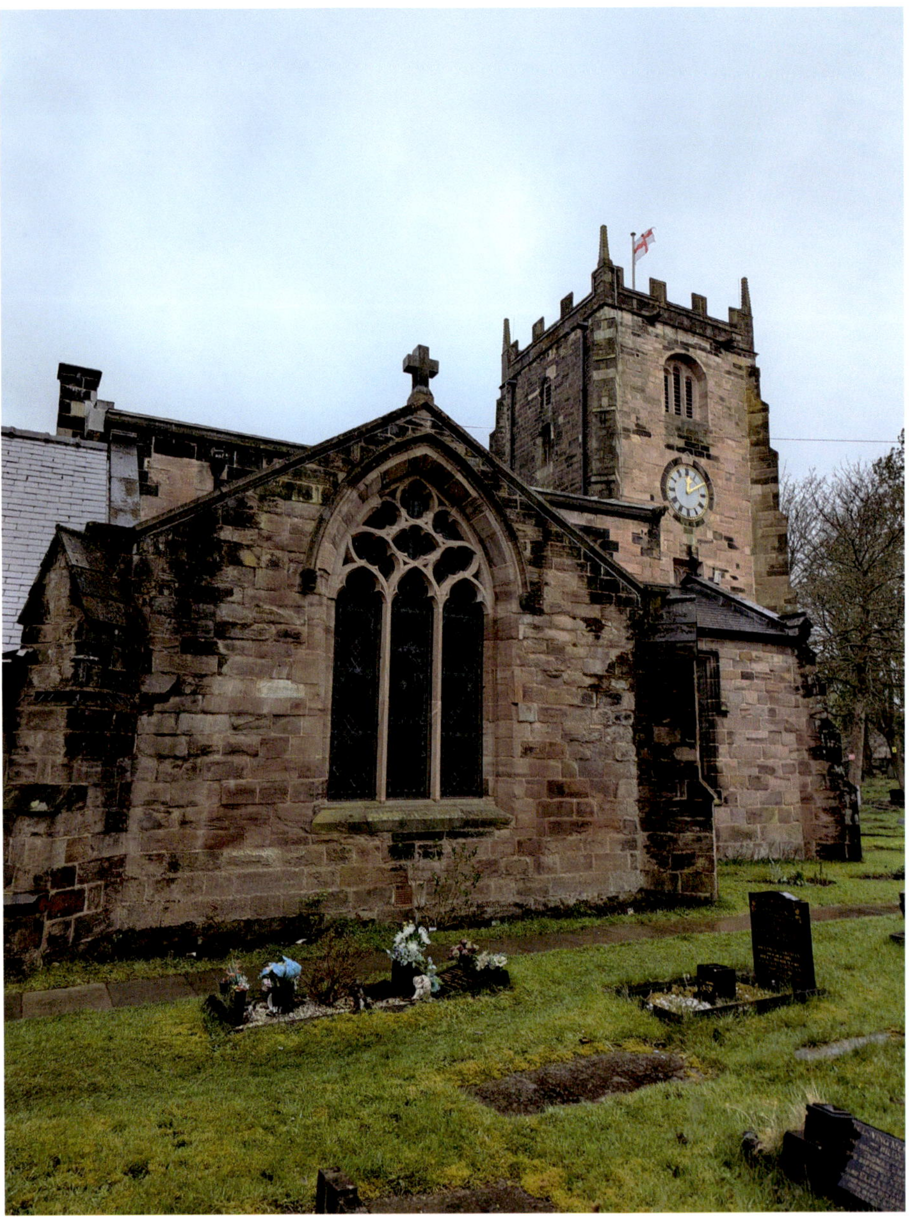

St Mary's Church, Radcliffe.

St Mary's Church has some notable stained glass by firms such as Shrigley and Hunt of Lancaster, William Wailes of Newcastle, and Heaton, Butler and Bayne of London, whose work also appears in St Ann's Church in Manchester city centre. The west window of the south aisle is by Willford of Stockport and dates to 1955. Willford's studio at Marple Bridge oversaw the repair of numerous war-damaged windows in the twentieth century.

33. ROCHDALE, ST CHAD

Much like Manchester Cathedral, St Chad's stands on a sandstone 'bluff' known locally as Sparrow Hill, although the scene is far more dramatic here in Rochdale with the Roch valley to the north and an exciting skyline with good views of the Victorian town hall.

As with other medieval churches in Greater Manchester, St Chad's is almost entirely embattled, but what sets it apart from other churches is its extraordinary length and detached pinnacles. The church has a six-bay nave and a six-bay chancel, which is something only encountered elsewhere in Greater Manchester at Manchester Cathedral. In height, the Victorian chancel is slightly greater than the nave, but it is important to note that until 1873 a prospect of the church and churchyard would have looked dramatically different to the building and setting we see today. In 1873, architect W. H. Crossland added a Perpendicular belfry stage to the top of the medieval tower as well as a new south porch. In 1884 work began under the instruction of architect Joseph Stretch Crowther to rebuild the chancel. Both architects employed Thomas Earp to adorn the church with large stone gargoyles, grotesques and characterful carvings on the string course beneath the parapet. These are worthy of individual inspection for their skill and playfulness. Truly eye-catching details to be admired.

The interior is in every way quite breathtaking. Prior to its restoration in the mid-nineteenth century, like so many of the larger town churches, St Chad's had an internal south gallery, box pews and a three-decker pulpit against one side of a north nave arcade pier, projecting into the central aisle. Of course, changes to the liturgical and architectural setting of Anglican worship in the nineteenth century removed such settings as the liturgy of the church was reformed. Today can be seen wide, three-light windows of the nave clerestory, which cast an enormous wash of light upon the central worship space and the nave roof rebuilt in 1854 and 1855. The removal of the old pews and their replacement with non-upholstered chairs in the nave and nave aisles should not deter exploration of the collegiate-style chancel where a rich repository of earlier church woodwork survives, including screens, stalls and priest's seats, although in some cases they have been recycled. The carved choir stalls are unlike any other in a parish church in Greater Manchester and cannot be missed. The western most stalls date from the nineteenth century, with those on the east end dating to the fifteenth century. The older are said to come from Canterbury (Kent), but the details of their acquisition and reconstitution here are not widely known. Carved bench ends depicting figures and beasts include a double-headed fish, glaring and snarling animals, an armed knight with a heraldic shield, and priests knelt in prayer.

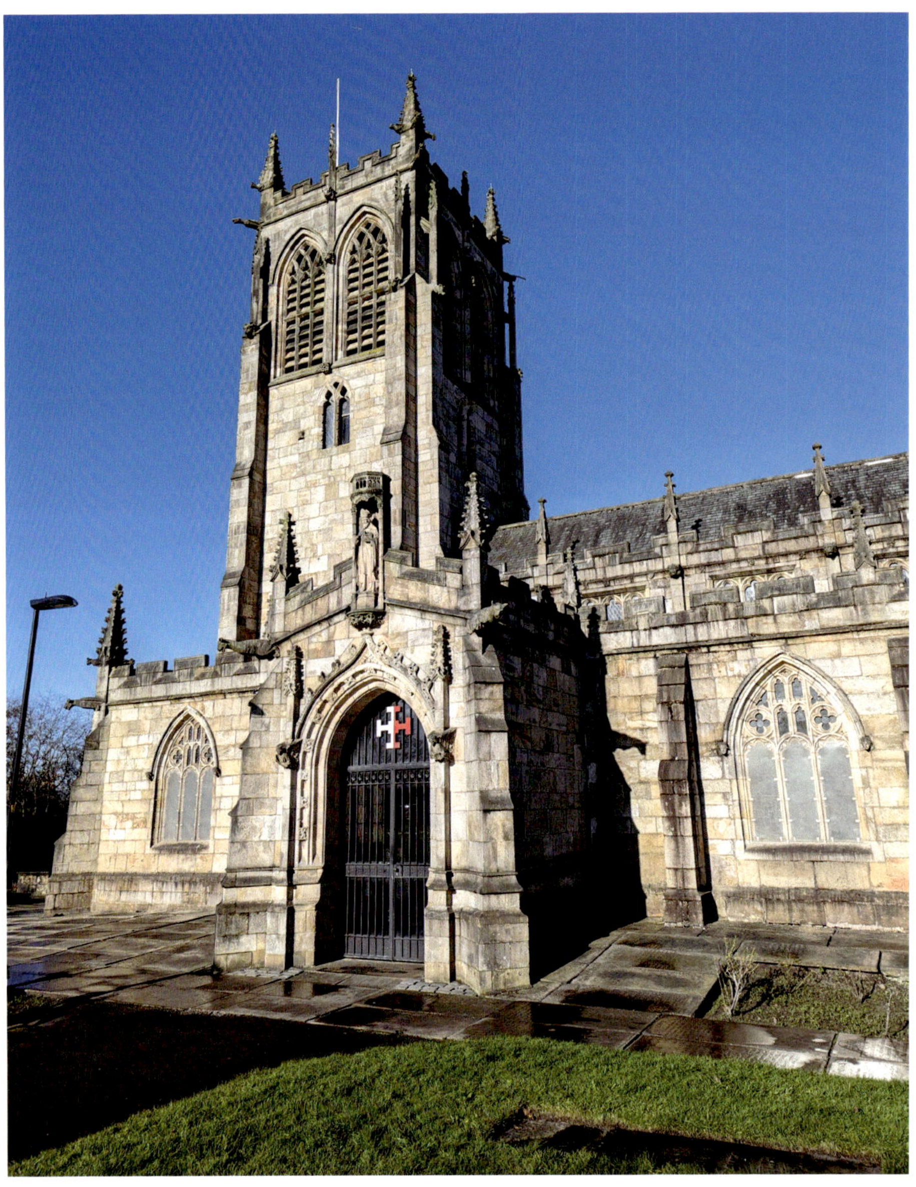

St Chad's, Rochdale.

Look up at the hammerbeam chancel ceiling. One would be entirely forgiven for thinking this is early work, but it is also Victorian in date.

There are some fine stained-glass windows to be seen when walking around the building. One of the best is a window of superb quality across three lights depicting scenes from the life of St Chad designed by the firm James Powell & Son, or Whitefriars Glass, dating to the 1930s. Two scenes depict St Chad preaching at Rochdale and St Chad telling his brethren of his vision. Another notable window is

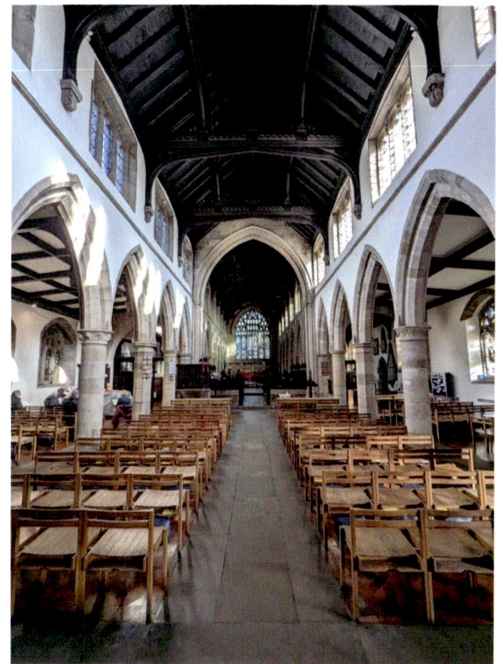

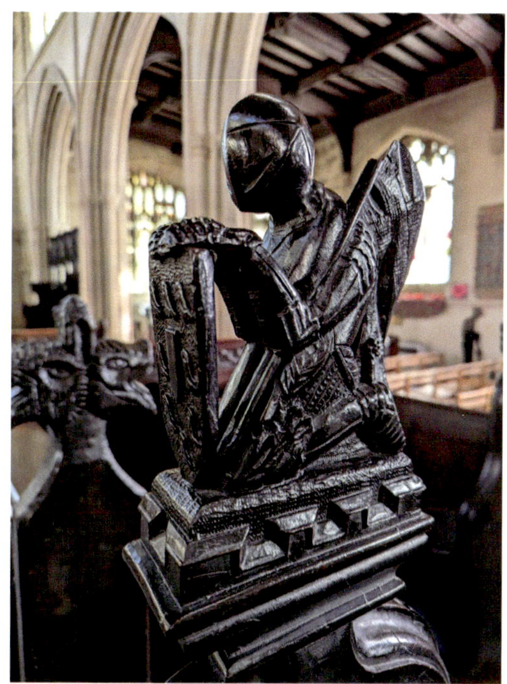

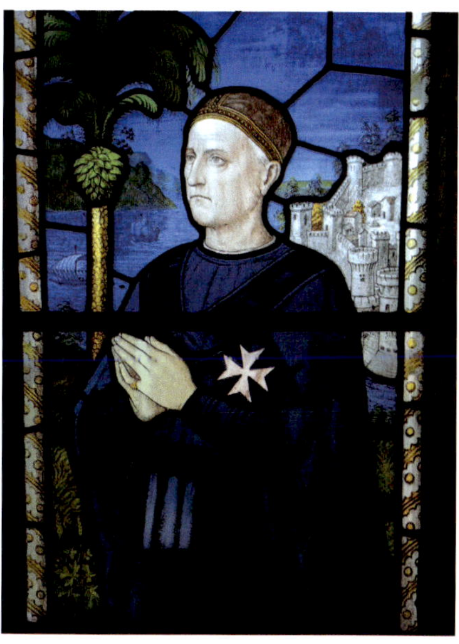

Above left: Interior of St Chad's, looking east.

Above right: Choir stall detail, St Chad's.

Right: Sir Clement Royds's stained-glass window, St Chad's.

one depicting Archangel Michael with a large figure of local politician Sir Clement Royds knelt in prayer to one side wearing a very specific costume and insignia. The window was installed to the glory of God and in memory of Sir Clement Royds, Knight of Justice of the Order of St John of Jersusalm in England. Royds was a soldier and Conservative MP for Rochdale from 1895 to 1906.

34. ROCHDALE, ST MARY IN THE BAUM

St Mary in the Baum is an unusual dedication, and it is said that 'baum' in the local dialect refers to the wildflowers growing in the meadows where the church was built. It is almost beyond belief today to think that St Mary's was a chapel which opened for worship in 1742 amongst an area of fields for the cure of souls of those living north of the river Roch away from the medieval parish church in Rochdale. The land on which it was built was gifted by Samuel Chetham of Castleton Hall. The original architect of the chapel is not known, but in design it was a utilitarian brick built, preaching box of six bays with round-headed windows. There was little of great architectural significance about it at all until the turn of the twentieth century when it was agreed to rebuild the chapel instead of building a brand new church. It is architect Ninian Comper's masterful reordering and decoration of the former chapel between 1909 and 1911, which makes this church so special and of significant architectural appeal. The ground plan consists chiefly of two main aisles and the high altar is in the south aisle, a wise decision as it maximised the income of natural light through the large Perpendicular windows, added by Comper.

A richly decorated and finely carved wooden screen, designed by Comper, separates the nave from the chancel. The screen has tracery and tabernacles containing saints, each holding symbols of their martyrdom or ministry. Positioned above the screen is a group depicting the crucified Christ flanked by the Blessed Virgin Mary, St John, and two angels; above Christ. It is possible to walk on this screen with access from the organ loft and console. The south nave aisle ceiling above was once highly decorated but the finish is deteriorating and in need of conservation.

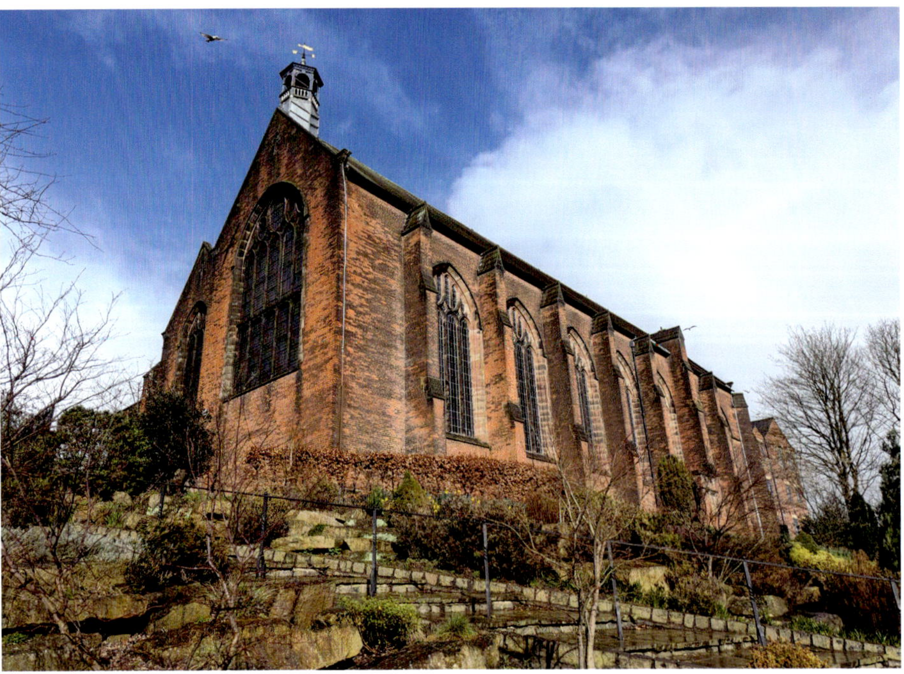

St Mary in the Baum, Rochdale.

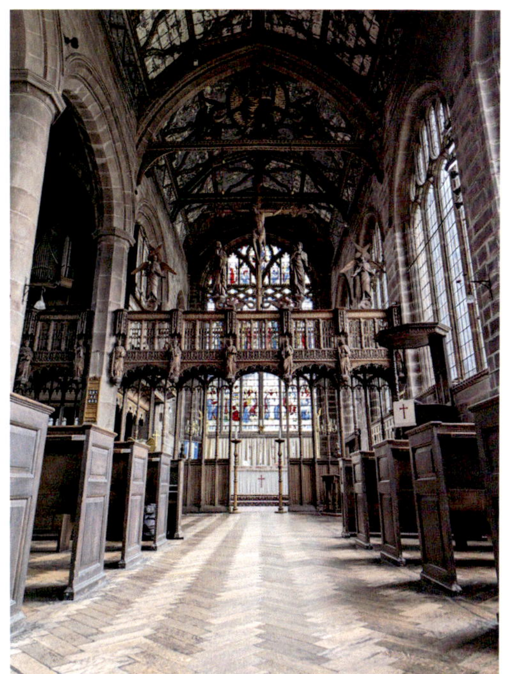

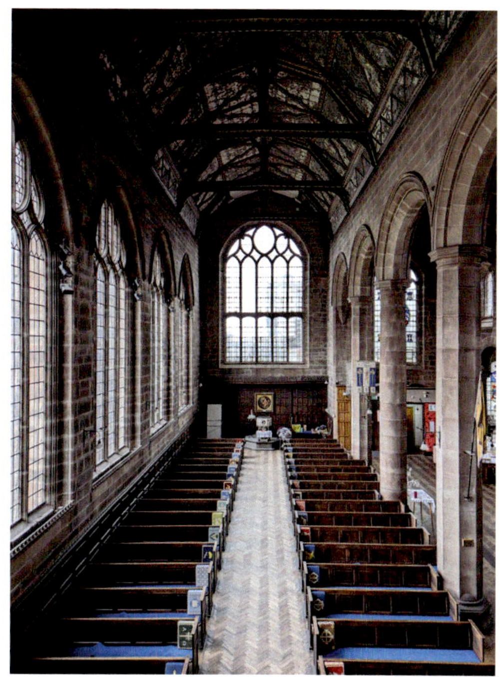

Above left: Interior of St Mary in the Baum, Rochdale, looking east.

Above right: Interior of St Mary in the Baum, looking west from the chancel screen platform.

Right: East window viewed from the chancel screen platform, St Mary in the Baum.

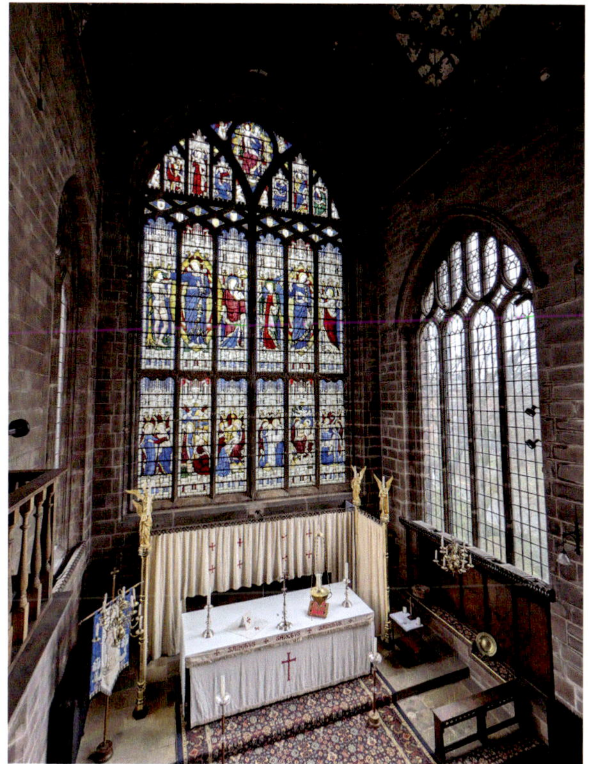

A church leaflet which circulated when the church opened for worship following Comper's refurbishment specifically sought to attract the working class of Rochdale: 'We want Lancashire men and women in their working-clothes, in their clogs and shawls, to be constantly coming into the Church at all times, so that we may help to break down the false idea that Churchgoing is a duty for Sunday alone, and that it is only meant for people in their best clothes.'

There is a great deal more to see inside, including stained glass designed by Comper himself. A series of stained-glass roundels dating back to 1867 were re-set in groups of three in the windows of the northern aisle. This is one of the most spectacular churches in Greater Manchester and must be seen to be believed.

35. SALFORD CATHEDRAL

Salford Cathedral, officially known as the Cathedral Church of St. John the Evangelist, is regarded as one of the finest Roman Catholic churches of the first half of the nineteenth century, built between 1844 and 1848. It joins the ranks of numerous other remarkable Victorian Roman Catholic churches in Manchester. The cathedral church was designed by Matthew Ellison Hadfield, a Gothic Revival architect known for his work on Roman Catholic churches. Inspiration for the architectural elevations were drawn from masterpieces of authentic Gothic design to be seen in England. The west façade (though it actually faces south) and the nave were designed as smaller versions of the façade at Howden Minster

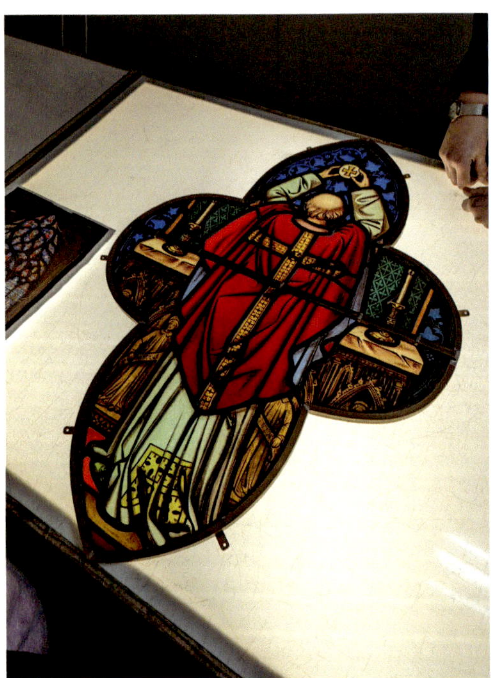
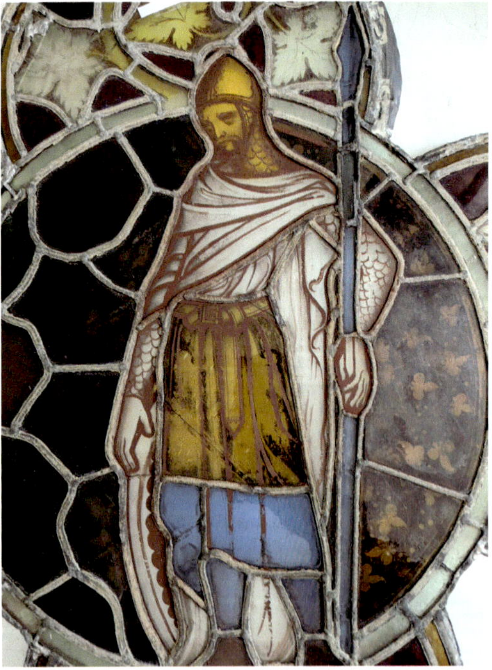

Above left and above right: Salford Cathedral stained-glass window in the studio for conservation at Bailey Studios.

(East Riding of Yorkshire) while the choir and sanctuary take their inspiration from Selby Abbey (North Yorkshire). As for the tower and spire, these were inspired by the design of St Mary Magdalene's Church in Newark-on-Trent (Nottinghamshire).

The cathedral was undergoing extensive restoration at the time of writing and had been closed from 2022 to at least July 2025. The restoration focused on both the interior and on the exterior of the cathedral. It has been completely re-roofed with repointing works to the stonemasonry and soaring spire. The altar has been relocated closer to its original position under the central tower crossing and there has been an extensive redecoration of the entire interior.

A full conservation of the Victorian stained glass in the windows was also undertaken. This saw the removal of the glazing to Barely Studios in Dunnington (North Yorkshire) for cleaning. The stained glass has been modified and returned to site to be installed within an environmental protective glazing scheme, protecting the glass from decay in the future.

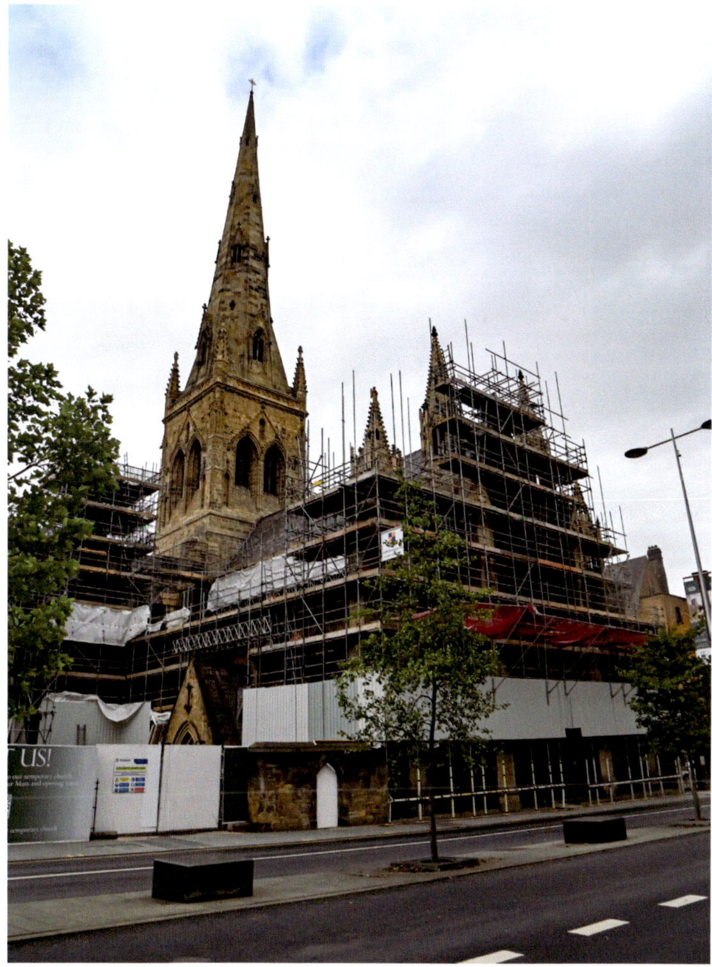

Salford Cathedral. (Courtesy of Jenna Johnston)

36. SALFORD, ST PHILIP

St Philip's is a neoclassical 'Commissioners' church' built in 1825 and designed by architect Sir Robert Smirke, friend of Lord Elgin and the architect of the British Museum. It is a perfect late Georgian town church with a slick tower and Ionic portico. This was once the church's main entrance but has today been relocated to the door of the entrance. Smirke is noted for reusing his design for St Mary's Church, Bryanston Square, London. The tower design was also employed at Wandsworth's church dedicated to St Anne also in London. A Commissioners' church (sometimes known as a 'Waterloo church') is the name given to a type

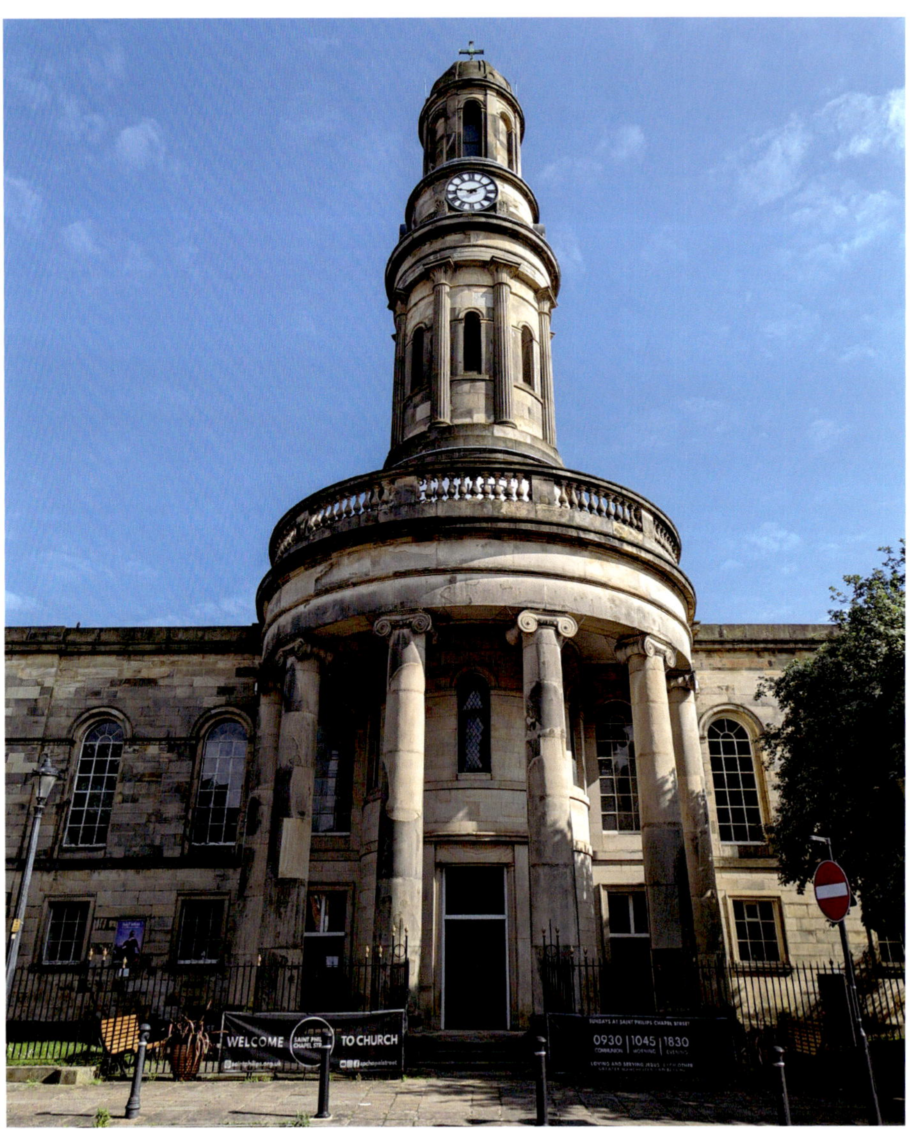

St Philip's Church, Salford.

of new church built in the early nineteenth century using funds granted by Parliament. These churches were commissioned under the Church Building Acts, particularly the Church Building Act of 1818 which funded new Anglican churches in response to rapid population growth at the start of the century.

The church sits on St Philip's Place with views of a wide south elevation facing Chapel Street further west on the road from Salford Roman Catholic Cathedral. When the church was built in the first half of the 19th century, it was intended to serve the double purpose of parish church for a well-to-do residential district and garrison church for the military barracks on Regent Road.

37. SALFORD, SACRED TRINITY

Tucked within the heart of Salford stands Sacred Trinity Church. A squat church with a splendid west tower added in 1635 when the church was founded by Humphrey Booth, a respected local merchant whose vision laid the foundation for the neat church we see today. By 1650, it had earned the full designation of a parish church, quickly becoming a centre of spiritual and civic activity. In 1733, the great preacher John Wesley addressed a crowd within its walls. Walls which have changed significantly since it was first built in the seventeenth century.

The main body was rebuilt in 1751 in a Georgian style which is quite different in architectural style than the earlier west tower, reflecting the tastes of both periods. Later, in the early 20th century, the sanctuary and east end were redesigned. Additionally, a new porch and vestry were added to the south-east corner.

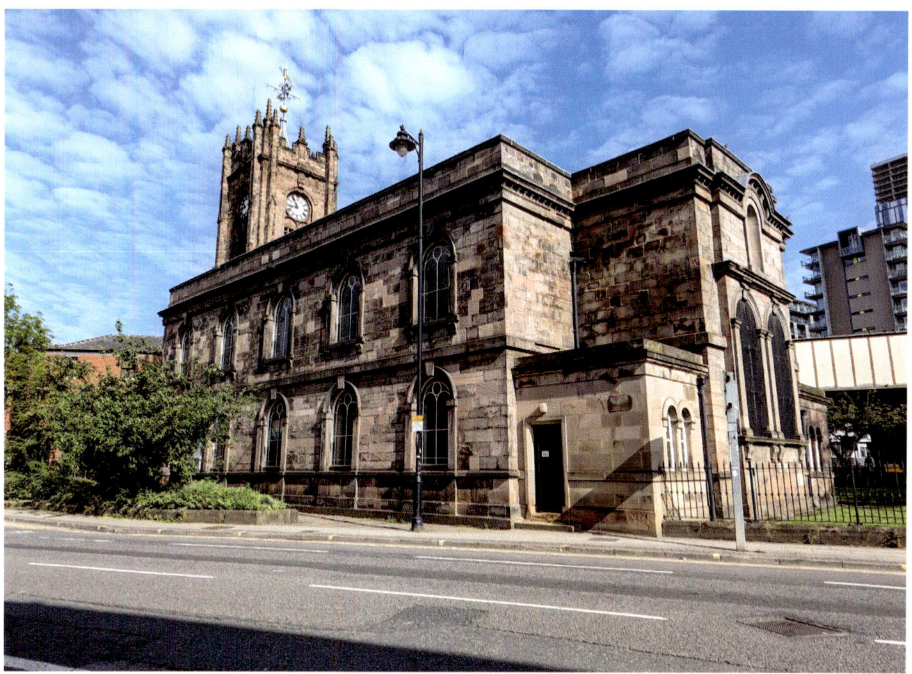

Sacred Trinity Church, Salford.

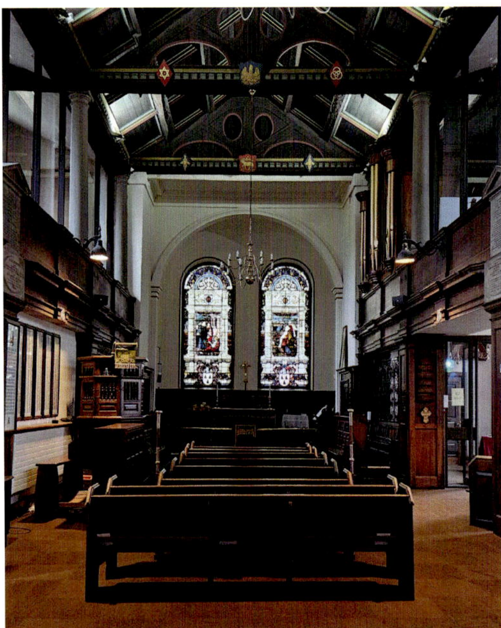
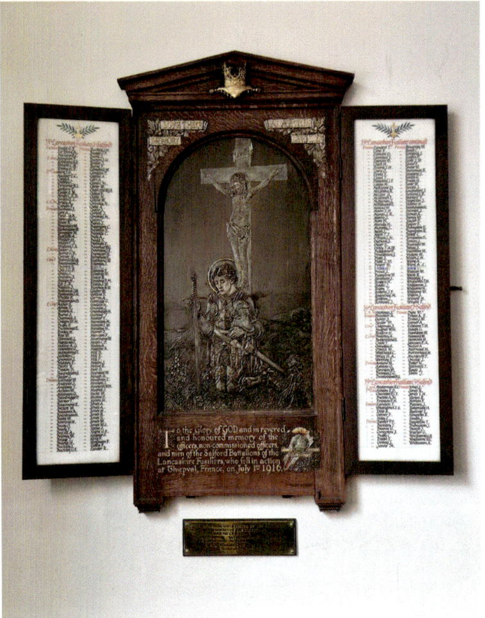

Above left: Sacred Trinity Church, Salford. (Courtesy of Simon Knott)

Above right: War memorial at Sacred Trinity. (Courtesy of Simon Knott)

In the 1840s, as the new railway lines threatened to cut through Salford, the church found itself directly in the path of the new Victoria station. Remarkably, the course of the proposed railway line was forced to reroute so that the church could remain and as such it avoided demolition. A more modern transformation came in 1980, when the interior was sensitively remodelled to include toilets, offices, and greater flexibility for a growing range of uses.

Inside, the church holds treasures that speak of its long legacy. The altar, chairs and lectern, all dating back to 1690. The Jacobean pulpit, crafted in 1700, is said to have once slid on a runner into the centre of the nave so even those in the gallery could see and hear the Minister and orator of the day delivering a sermon. There is a fine wall-mounted war memorial with a central plaque depicting a kneeling soldier in antique costume before Christ, dedicated to the Glory of God and in revered and honoured memory of the officers, non-commissioned officers, and men of the Salford battalions of the Lancashire Fusiliers who fell in action at Thiepval, France, on 1 July 1916.

38. STOCKPORT, ST MARY

Stockport is located in the historic county of Cheshire, and the Lancashire boundary runs immediately north of the town centre, following the River Mersey and M60 motorway as a rough visual marker. The Metropolitan Borough of Stockport was created in 1974. Very little of medieval Stockport remains to be seen in surviving architecture of the modern town. The heritage centre in St Mary's Church, staffed on open days by volunteers, is a remarkable resource to better understand the heritage of Stockport going back to the later medieval period, although the evolution of the old township of Stockport and its modern, metropolitan development are perhaps best experienced on foot through the perambulations. Brutalist buildings of the past century mix in the metropolitan centre with buildings of the nineteenth and eighteenth centuries. Some earlier buildings survive along the course of what is described as the town's one tremendous asset, its marketplace. Here, the difference in levels between

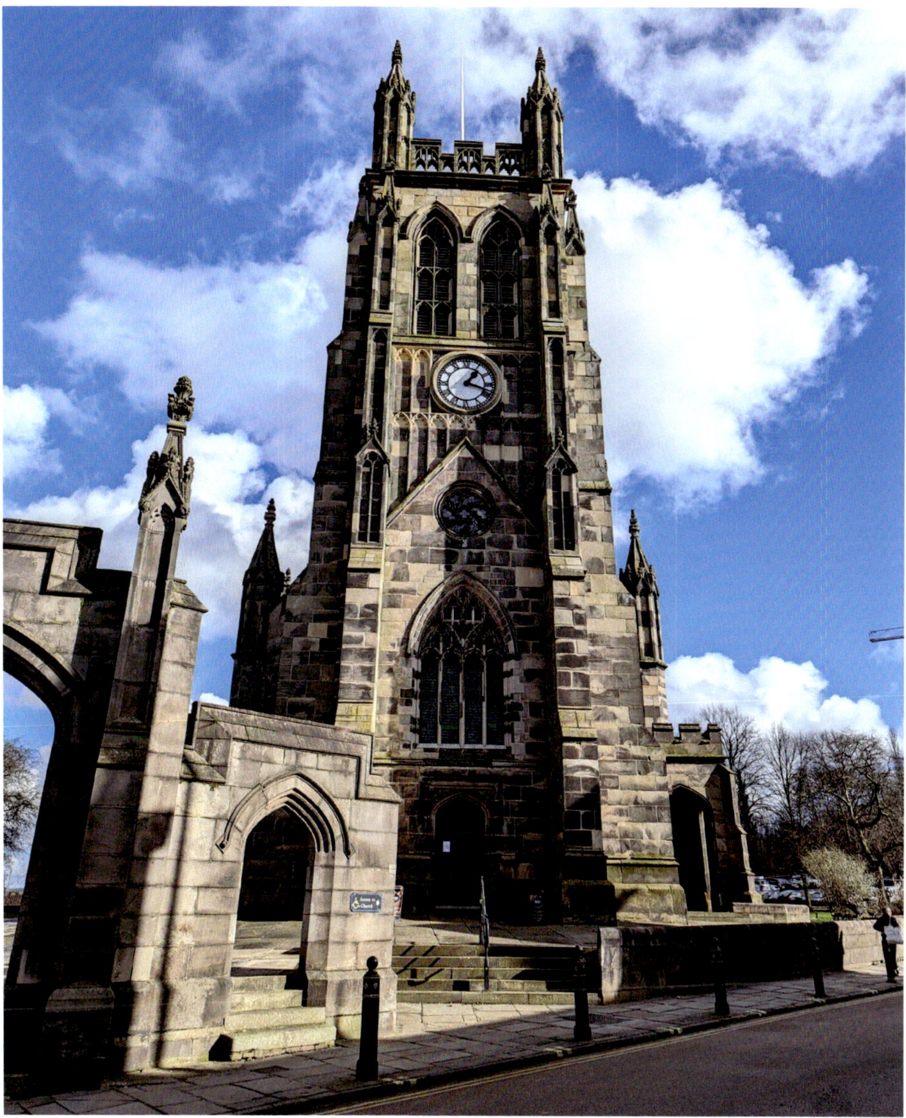

St Mary's, Stockport.

the marketplace and the lower underbanks in the northern part of the town are impressive. Beneath deep staircases and meandering alleys, the River Mersey flows hidden beneath the marketplace. Standing immediately east of the ancient marketplace, opposite the Victorian Market Hall, a glass superstructure with timber cladding and cast-iron interior features, is St Mary's Parish Church.

Secondary sources generally agree that St Mary's Church has its origins in the twelfth century. No physical or structural evidence of the first church building on, or very close to this site, survives. Only the fourteenth century chancel, which remains as one of the principal medieval structures of the old town. This is constructed in red Cheshire sandstone. It is surprisingly durable, even after centuries of exposure, but appears quite coarsely grained in places and is easy to rub off with your fingers. Stones quarried since are of a much finer grain quality and the aesthetic difference between old and replacement masonry is quite distinct.

St Mary's Church can be visited outside of regular service times. The church has a community café on Saturdays and the Stockport Heritage Centre, located at the end of the north chancel aisle, which is regularly open to the public. Stepping through the west entrance opposite the market and into the nave, the church is clearly not medieval, if that was not already apparent from the elevation of the late Georgian Gothic tower, scaling 95 feet in height. Structural defects in the tower and a general desire for a new, more spacious nave, led to the rebuilding of the main body of the old church between 1813 and 1817 to designs by architect Lewis Wyatt. Further improvements were made in 1882 under the oversight of architect Joseph Stretch

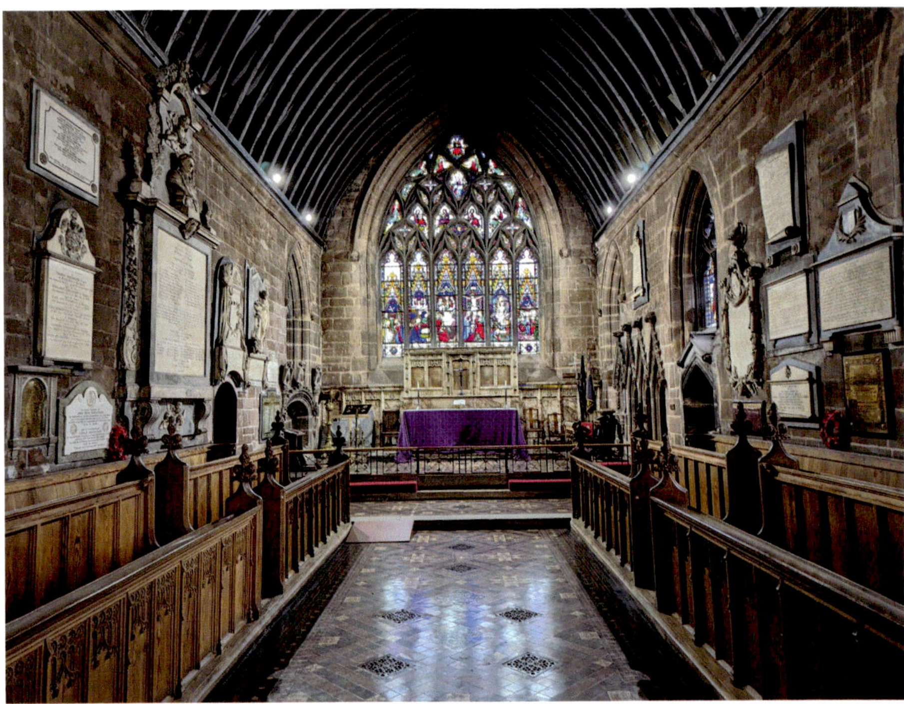

Chancel, interior looking east, St Mary's, Stockport.

Crowther, including the provision of larger windows, permitting more natural light, and the eye-catching chancel arch with traceried panels bearing the royal coat of arms of George III. This dates from the time of Wyatt's previous rebuilding of the church and is purported to be the largest royal coat of arms in an English parish church. A major reordering of the church between 2007 and 2015 transformed the interior into the space we see today. St Mary's is proud of the fact that despite building work taking place over several years, the building only closed for one month in February 2013 when the floor was renewed.

The fourteenth-century chancel has been heavily restored but is of interest to visitors looking for a step back in time to Stockport of the Middle Ages. The east window is perhaps a copy of what may have been there, and it attempts to uphold the Gothic character of its predecessor through a lively tracery and does so admirably on scale alone. The south chancel aisle windows were also renewed, although you can see the scars of the originals which were clearly slightly larger. To the north side there is a choir vestry built in 1882, next to the clergy vestry with a small oratory to the east side which was part of the original fourteenth-century church. There was also a side chapel dedicated to Richard de Vernon, rector from 1304 to 1334, on the south side of the chancel which was demolished in 1882. Richard de Vernon's stone effigy was presumably removed from his chapel and placed under the existing burial niche in the north wall of the sanctuary, itself adapted in the seventeenth century when it contained a different effigy belonging to a different family altogether.

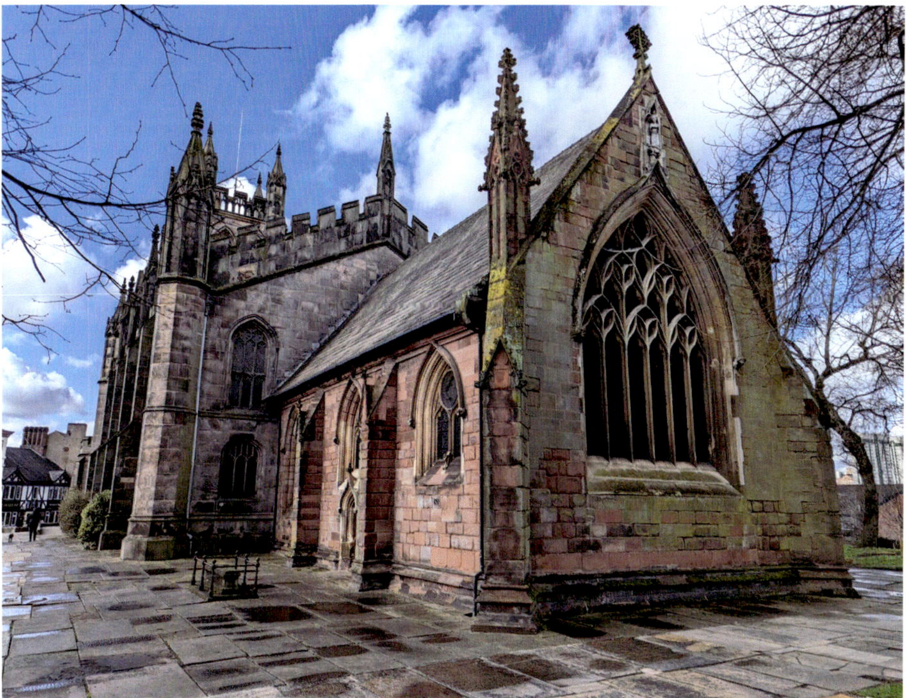

Chancel exterior, St Mary's, Stockport.

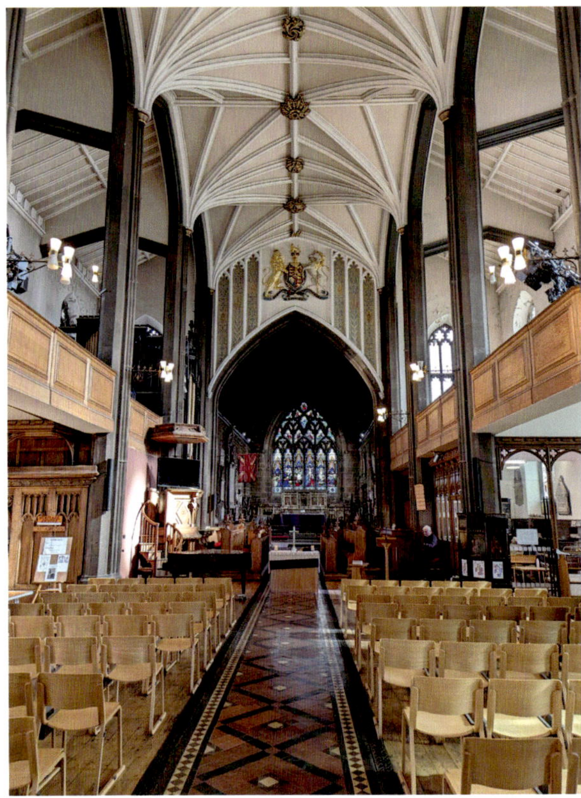

Nave of St Mary's,
interior looking east.

The chancel has a late medieval roof, more typical of southern English traditions. The church visitor guidebook says it is easily overlooked, which is in part because it doesn't look more than 200 years old at all and has survived remarkably well. St Mary's Church has responded to its calling that it must contribute in an important way to the activity and inclusion of the busy marketplace. The church is fully accessible and staffed by welcoming and friendly volunteers.

39. STOCKPORT, ST PETER

St Peter's Church was built in 1768 at the expense of William Wright of Mottram Hall, near Prestbury. Designed in the Georgian Gothic style with a prominent west tower, it was consecrated in May 1768 by Bishop Edmund Keene of Chester. St Peter's Church is constructed or faced in Flemish bonded brick with a wide preaching-box-style nave and a later chancel built in 1888. The tower is in three stages, with a round-headed window above the west door and an octagonal turret belfry stage at the top. The foundation stone bore the motto 'To the Glory of God and for the Good of Mankind', though its current location is unknown. Originally situated on the outskirts of Stockport, the church was constructed to serve a growing industrial population, but is now surrounded by more modern, largely twentieth-century buildings. At the time of writing, St Peter's is on Historic

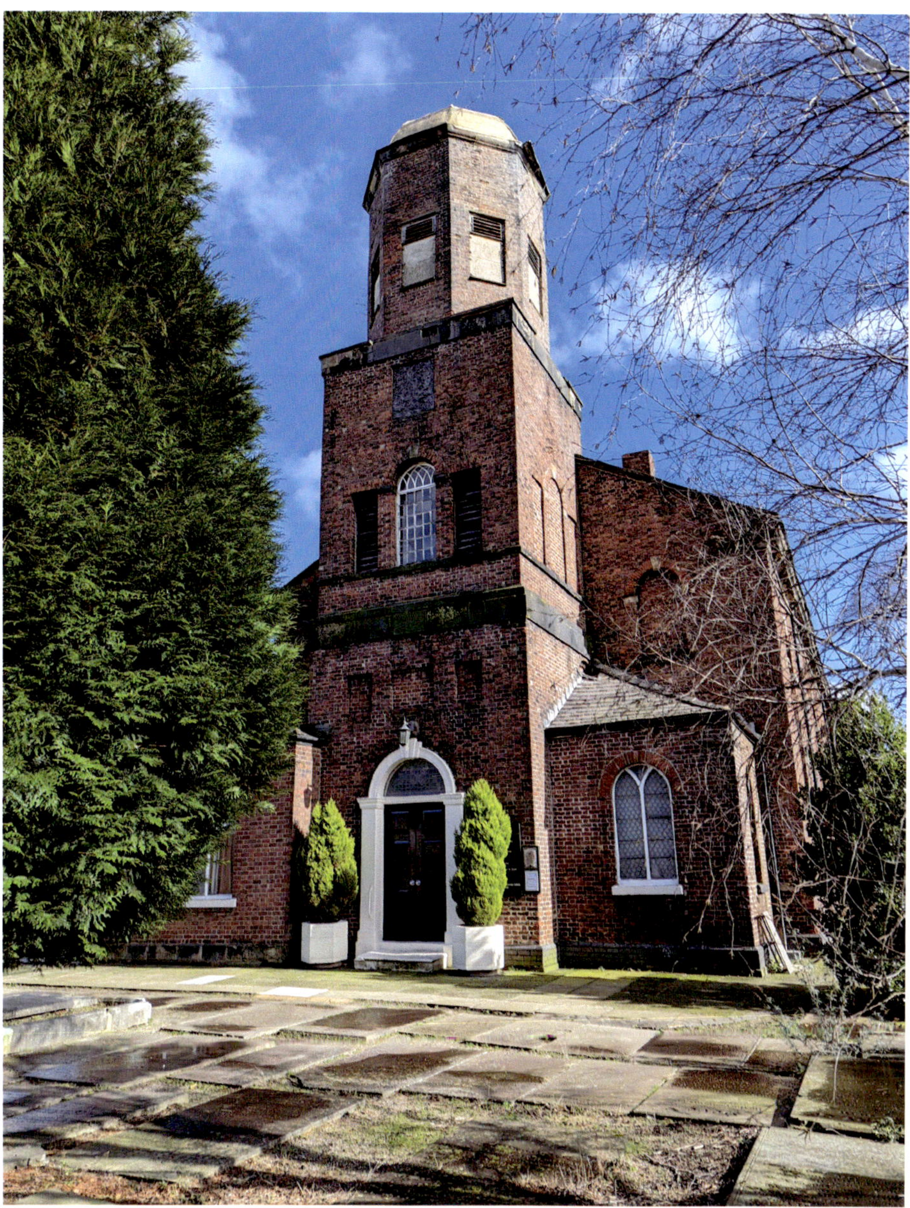

St Peter's, Stockport.

England's Heritage at Risk register due to extensive problems including water ingress at high level. There is cracking to eaves level stonework and vegetation growth can be seen in the same areas. Water ingress is reportedly due to the roof being in generally poor condition, with slipped roof slates and defective roof timbers behind rainwater goods. It is hoped that this church can be returned to good health following extensive repairs.

40. Wythenshawe, William Temple Church

Sitting in a large, gated churchyard in suburban Wythenshawe, William Temple Church is a significant example of post-war ecclesiastical architecture, designed to be congruous with nearby housing and being built a time when new flat buildings built by Manchester County Borough Council and a new IT centre for Barclays Bank were established. Designed by architect George G. Pace, the church was constructed between 1964 and 1965 and is highly regarded by modernists for its architectural value. The church is dedicated to William Temple, a prominent Anglican bishop who served as Bishop of Manchester and Archbishop of both York and Canterbury between 1929 until his death in 1944. Temple was known for his contributions to social justice, education and theological scholarship, and so a church dedicated in his name serving as a place of worship for Christians and other faiths and community engagement is fitting.

The church's modernist design reflects the principles of the mid-twentieth-century architecture, characterised by Pace's favoured use of clean, solid lines, material and form. One of Pace's briefs was to consider the acoustics with a view that music being performed there would be fundamental. The steep roof has inset dormer windows, and the interior is supported by black-painted steel girders, a practical solution necessitated by the wet ground conditions at the site. Pace's design emphasises a non-traditional, liturgical arrangement with a central altar and seating arranged for communal worship. Notably, Pace asked that no plaques be placed on the interior walls, adhering to his philosophy that churches should be built solely for the glory of God.

The pews were brought from closed churches in and around Greater Manchester, much in the same way they were not designed new at Pace's church in Chadderton.

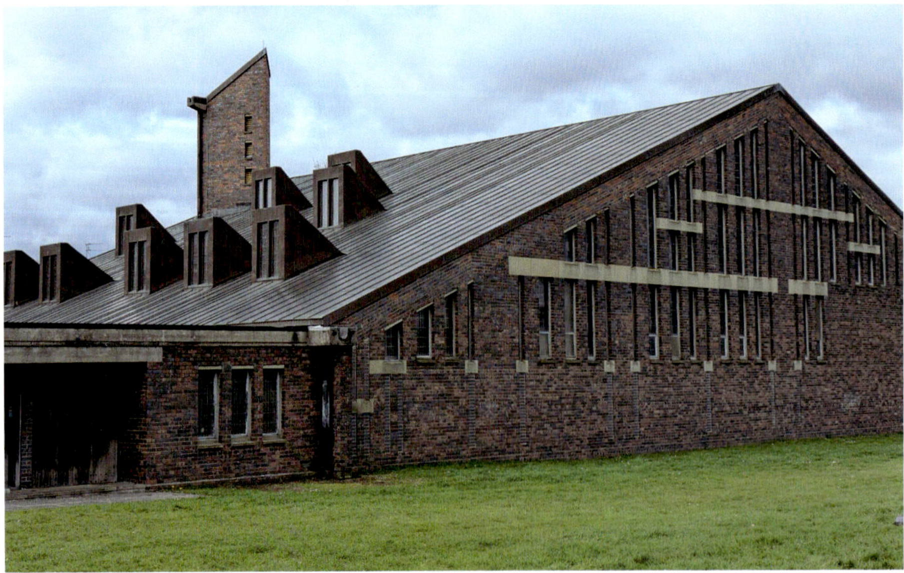

William Temple Church, Wythenshawe.